Let me start out by saying, you really have to get this book, *From Wilderness to Wonders*! Why? Because if you've not gone through a wilderness experience in your walk with the Lord, you are likely to do so sometime in the future. And Katherine's experiences and wisdom will be a God-send to you. And if you've already emerged from that dark night of the soul season, this book will *finally* help you make sense out of what that season was all about!

But listen to me. As I read this book and got closer and closer to the end, I said to myself, "This isn't just about the wilderness experience. This book is literally about how to live the Christian life in Christ!" It has everything—and so much of it is in story form, my favorite kind of writing. The stories and sections on forgiveness, frankly, are worth the cost of the book all by themselves. Forgiveness is one of the hardest parts of the Christian walk, and this book "nails it" on forgiveness.

Are you having a hard time forgiving someone? Get this book!

Want to know how to walk with God throughout your life? Get this book!

Want to know how to speed up the *process* of this *wilderness* season? *Get this book!*

—STEVE SHULTZ
FOUNDER, THE ELIJAH LIST AND BREAKING CHRISTIAN NEWS

The wilderness is a place all Christians will go through as we move from glory to glory, but it doesn't have to be a dry season filled with negative experiences. In her newest book, *From Wilderness to Wonders*, Katherine Ruonala does an outstanding job of pointing out another aspect of the wilderness experience—the process between promise, calling, and fulfillment. It is in this place that we have the glorious opportunity to lean on Jesus and discover the deep things of His Holy Spirit.

I strongly recommend this book to equip you to embrace the journey with fresh hope and perspective.

—Dr. Ché Ahn
Apostle, Harvest Apostolic Center
Founding Pastor, HRock Church, Pasadena, California
President, Harvest International Ministry

As believers, many of those who are yet to fulfill their calling go through a wilderness experience of some form during their lifetime. The Scriptures tell us that God doesn't tempt us, but He can test our character.

Through my own wilderness journey I've learned that once we change our thinking from living in the natural to living in the spiritual mind, we regain greater access to unseen spiritual realities. We need to use this time in the wilderness as a time of strengthening and preparation for greater things God has in store for us.

I've known Katherine for many years now, and I know that she has written from her own experiences of what it means to pay the price before entering into the arena of success. She is not only a prophet but also an inspirational healing revivalist who has inspired many. I believe this book, *From Wilderness to Wonders*, will impart revelation and understanding to every believer.

—Adam F. Thompson
Co-Planter, Field of Dreams Australia,
WWW.VOICEOFFIREMINISTRIES.ORG
Coauthor, *The Divinity Code to Understanding Your Dreams and Visions*
Author, *The Supernatural Man*

Reading through Katherine Ruonala's book *From Wilderness to Wonders* was like finding buried treasure! This book will provide amazing insights into the process God takes each of us through to make us more like Christ and to make us useful instruments in His hand. You will find a map for your life journey as Katherine walks us through the divine process of finding God's wonders in every wilderness experience. God will open up something beautiful and marvelous within you as you go through this unique book. Read it for fresh insights! Read it for gaining wisdom! It will change your life!

—Dr. Brian Simmons
Lead Translator, The Passion Translation Project

Have you ever received a prophetic word from God and then wondered, "How is it going to come to pass?" Have you ever gotten discouraged during your process of walking out God's call on your life? Then you have to read Katherine Ruonala's new book, *From Wilderness to Wonders*! We all have a private journey in God, and when we compare ourselves to others it's easy to grow discouraged and frustrated. In this book you will learn how to successfully navigate the process of fulfilling God's plan for your life and actually enjoy the journey. Katherine shares life-changing insights from God's Word and from her own private journey into the amazing prophetic miracle ministry God has given her. This is a great book that I know will help a lot of people! You will be truly inspired.

—Matt Sorger
Prophetic Healing Evangelist
Founder, Matt Sorger Ministries
Author, *Power for Life: Keys to a Life Marked by the Presence of God*
www.mattsorger.com

This is a gold mine of revelation that will lead to transformation. Read this book, then let it read you. *From Wilderness to Wonders* contains everything you need to take you from glory to glory. No matter who you are, no matter where you are, a good guide makes all the difference. Katherine proves that after the test there is a testimony.

—Leif Hetland
President, Global Mission Awareness
Author, *Seeing Through Heaven's Eyes*

FROM
WILDERNESS
to
Wonders

KATHERINE
RUONALA

CHARISMA
HOUSE

FROM WILDERNESS TO WONDERS by Katherine Ruonala
Published by Charisma House
Charisma Media/Charisma House Book Group
600 Rinehart Road
Lake Mary, Florida 32746
www.charismahouse.com

Copyright © 2015 by Katherine Ruonala
All rights reserved

Visit the author's website at www.katherineruonala.com.

Cover design by Lisa Rae McClure
Design Director: Justin Evans

Library of Congress Cataloging-in-Publication Data:
Ruonala, Katherine.
  From wilderness to wonders / Katherine Ruonala. -- First edition.
    pages cm
  ISBN 978-1-62998-614-2 (trade paper) -- ISBN 978-1-62998-615-9 (e-book)

1. Christian life. 2. Wilderness (Theology) 3. Providence
and government of God--Christianity. 4. Consolation. I.
Title.
  BV4509.5.R8635 2015
  248.8'6--dc23

                                    2015027439

First edition

15 16 17 18 19 — 987654321
Printed in the United States of America

To my children, Jessica, Emily, and Joseph.

Each one of you fills my heart with more joy than I can express. It is my prayer that your life journeys will be filled with continuous joy and that you will experience the delight of fellowship with God in ever-increasing ways.

And to all those on the journey between promise and fulfillment, may you find hope and joy in the knowledge that God loves you, that He is for you and is making all things work together for your good.

CONTENTS

ACKNOWLEDGMENTS

*T*O MY WONDERFUL husband, Tom, for your patient, loving, selfless, and wise support as we have walked through these journeys together. I love you and thank God continually for you.

To all our Glory City Church families, pastors, and leaders, I love you! Thank you for your love and for celebrating God's goodness with me as we press on to see the message of God's great love transform the world.

To Helen Cobanov, Chris Turner, Emily Harland, Sarah Cheesman, Ron Fearneyhough, Kelly Horne, and Chris Wyman—thank you for your help in the editing process. I am so blessed by your wonderful support, encouragement, and help.

To Chris Tiegreen for your help with the manuscript. I so value your friendship and support.

To my friend Sheila Williams—I love that God has so often given us the privilege of traveling together. Your encouragement and support continues to be such a blessing in my life.

FOREWORD

*M*Y FRIEND JIM Goll told me about a friend of his from Australia named Katherine Ruonala. He said she had the same anointing as Kathryn Kuhlman, which piqued my interest, because I knew Kathryn Kuhlman. Miss Kuhlman had the greatest healing ministry I had ever witnessed. So with that recommendation I told my producer to investigate, and we found that genuine, verified miracles follow Katherine Ruonala.

The rest is history. I invited her to be a guest on my television show, *It's Supernatural!*, and many were touched by the miraculous! Katherine truly has a miracle anointing like Miss Kuhlman. The presence of God flowing from her was tangible, and I would describe it as rivers of liquid love.

Perhaps that is why the theme of Katherine's new book, *From Wilderness to Wonders*, hit a big nerve with me. I thought about all the people who have believed God for a miracle, meditated on the Scriptures, prayed, fasted, and had many people with miracle ministries pray for them but have seen *no results*. Some have believed God for five or more years and yet they have not been healed. They still believe in miracles. They still believe in a healing Jesus but have given up on being healed themselves. After all those years, they smile and speak in faith, but deep in their heart, even if their mind won't admit it, they have lost hope.

This book is for them and anyone else who has started to give up on God's promises. It will jump-start hope and cause miracle-working faith to explode! The teaching and miracle testimonies in this book will restore child-like faith—just in time. It will build faith not only for your miracle but also for the "greater" miracles Jesus predicted and that the world is now positioned for.

My friend Kathryn Kuhlman saw this day. She said she saw a time when everyone in the hospital would be healed! I see football stadiums jammed packed with wor-shipping Christians. I see the glory of God invading, and in a minute everyone is healed! That day is almost here. You would not be reading this book if you were not chosen to carry God's healing power in the last of the last days. I pray the sweet presence of the Holy Spirit that accompa-nies Katherine's ministry will splash off these pages onto you and that you will never be the same!

—SID ROTH
HOST, *IT'S SUPERNATURAL!*

FOREWORD

ID YOU KNOW God has a dream in His heart? He wants the glory of the Lord to cover the earth as the waters cover the seas. He also has a personal plan and destiny for each one of our lives. God has massive global dreams, and our heavenly Father of Life also has very intimate, detailed dreams for each one of us!

We are each fearfully and wonderfully made. We are made in the image of God, and as born-again believers in the Lord Jesus Christ, there is a wonderful, God-breathed plan for our lives. But that plan often unfolds one chapter at a time. Oh my, but the adventure you and I are invited into—what a wonder-filled life awaits us!

In this comprehensive book, *From Wilderness to Wonders*, my friend and partner in ministry, Katherine Ruonala, takes us on a true-to-life journey of how to conceive the dream of God, bring it to birth, and nurture that prophetic calling into full maturation. Yes, it is a journey— a path less traveled. This road map does not include the typical fast-food concepts the Western world has allowed to seep into our "church culture." Katherine exposes these falsehoods and propels us to a realm of truth.

We are called to enforce the victory of Calvary and enter into spiritual battle in order to move from the place of "wilderness" into the supernatural reality of a life filled with "wonder." Yes, you and I are each called to live a life of wonders. We are to provoke others around us and make them "wonder."

As you move from learning the wisdom lessons of chapter 3, "Thriving in the Wilderness," to the ultimate consummation found in chapter 12, "Delighting in God," you will be given more than just tools for your tool belt! You will be given an invitation to dream with God.

Oh, what an honor it is to dream God's dreams! If you are up to that type of journey, then read on. This book might just spark faith in your heart that you too are destined to live a wonder-filled life!

With anticipation,

—Dr. James W. Goll
Founder, Encounters Network
International Director, Prayer Storm
Advisory Board Member, Compassion Acts,
International Best-Selling Author
www.jamesgoll.com

INTRODUCTION

*T*IME. THAT SPACE between planting and harvesting, between promise and fulfillment. Living in a world where we are widely accustomed to instant gratification, the concept of having to wait can be frustrating. Yet if we understand the purpose and potential of these times, we can learn to cooperate with God and enjoy the journey.

Many live with a sense of destiny and promise but struggle to see how it can be fulfilled in the light of their present circumstances. That can be a frustrating situation, especially when they see how God is already moving in the lives of others. It invites all sorts of questions: *Why not me? I know God has called me to greater things, so why do I feel stuck where I am? What am I doing wrong? When will God fulfill the promises He gave me?*

This is a very common experience, and it can be disorienting if we don't understand what God is doing or know how to respond to it. Some people call it a "wilderness," and for good reason. Like Joseph in Egypt, the Israelites on the way to the Promised Land, David in exile, and many other figures in Scripture, we are in the midst of a process between calling and fulfillment. We may not be wandering in an actual wilderness as many of these biblical figures did, but we can easily imagine how they felt. Through their experiences we are able to take hope in the truth that God will also bring us through whatever situation we may find ourselves in.

Jesus spent years waiting for God's timing in His life too. He didn't begin His ministry until He was about thirty (Luke 3:23), which means there were long years of waiting. He had a calling. He had vision. And He had God's promises, but He was not yet walking in the fullness of what God had called Him to do.

Jesus also had an actual wilderness experience:

> Jesus, being filled with the Holy Spirit, returned from the Jordan and was led by the Spirit into the wilderness, being tempted by the devil for forty days. During those days He ate nothing. And when they were ended, He was hungry. The devil said to Him, "If You are the Son of God..."
>
> —LUKE 4:1–3, MEV

The Holy Spirit actually led Jesus into a wilderness time. And this was right after the Father had declared that He was well pleased with Him! The wilderness was an opportunity for Jesus to question whether God really was pleased with Him—whether the Father really did care about Him and if He was truly for Him. Just as Adam and Eve in the garden were faced with the question, "Did God say...?" Jesus had the opportunity to solidify the reality that God had spoken and could be trusted, which was evidenced in His response to temptation when He quoted the words of God. In the wilderness we have the same opportunities to have our trust in God's words tested and solidified until they become like iron in our soul. (See Psalm 105:18–19.) The enemy came at Jesus in the wilderness with all sorts of temptations and distractions, doing everything he could to steer Jesus away from His purpose, distort His thinking, or question His identity. But when Jesus came out of the wilderness, He began ministering with power the world had never seen before.

A lot of Christian leaders and teachers are doing a great job equipping God's people for their calling, showing the way to walk in God's power, and casting vision. Not many talk about the process between promise and fulfillment or calling and destiny, so the wilderness can come as a shock to those who are unprepared.

I believe there is a great need in our time to understand the processes of God, the baptism of fire, and the joy and power of surrender. My personal journey included years of frustration and wondering what God was doing, but I learned to lean on Him in those times and came out with a relationship that could not be shaken. Whenever I teach on this, it seems to resonate with many people. Some remark on how rare it is to hear from speakers about their years of preparation and their behind-the-scenes stories of trials God has brought them through. Many are encouraged to know the process from wilderness to wonders.

I believe this book will equip you to embrace your journey with fresh hope and perspective. The message within these pages is that not only can you survive the seasons between promise and fulfillment; you can thrive in them. In fact, with the right kind of response, your wilderness season can become a time of accelerated growth and fruitfulness.

I hope that encourages you. Wilderness seasons are a great opportunity to lean on your Beloved and learn the deep things of His Spirit. You learn to anchor yourself in the One who gives you lasting joy. You learn to carry the peace of God in every situation because the Prince of Peace is within you. You learn not to let the wilderness or the enemy shape your identity because you find your identity entirely in Him.

In the wilderness we learn to dream God's dreams. We discover God as our source in every situation. We learn how to respond to temptation, injustice, and pain. We not only endure obstacles and storms; we become victorious in them and rise above them. In the wilderness we learn to recognize divine invitation and wage war with the promises God has given us. Regardless of what we are going through, in the wilderness we learn to find our delight in God alone.

God wants to be the glory and the lifter of your head in every situation (Ps. 3:3, KJV). No matter how difficult your circumstances may seem, He wants you to look up and see His glorious face. He wants to tell you how lovely, free, clean, and redeemed you are. God wants you to know you are the beloved apple of His eye and that He has created you to shine.

The wilderness cannot prevent you from shining. Jesus shone in His wilderness season, and you can too. Jesus's wilderness experience became one of His greatest victories. That can be your testimony too. You are destined to shine just as He does and to walk in His power, doing even greater works than He did. And even if you're in the midst of a wilderness, that can begin right now.

Chapter 1

DREAMING
GOD'S DREAMS

*I*T WAS A typical summer's day in Statesboro, Georgia. I was scheduled to speak at a conference called "Glory Explosion." I felt pressured, as I had in previous times of ministry, because I knew the expectation was great for people to receive the miracles they desperately needed. But the Lord in His grace and His mercy reassured me, as He had done previously, that He had called me for such a time as this and that the Holy Spirit would never let me down.

I remember walking in. People had brought their children from the hospital and their friends who didn't yet know the Lord in the hope that they might see and believe. As I began to preach, the Holy Spirit came over me, and I could see Him beginning to move on people's hearts. When He comes like that, I know He wants to move in a greater measure, so I realized it was time to begin praying for people.

It began with a woman who had pain in her legs. She had come to the meeting because her son had asked her to host a couple who had driven up from out of town. Although she did not know Jesus, she reluctantly opened up her home and brought the couple to the meeting. She had been through several broken marriages and was living in depression as an alcoholic. She would drink all through the day and night. She would basically wake up drinking. Having suffered for many years, she received a word of knowledge, and her legs were instantly healed. As she walked around in amazement, testing out her legs, she came back asking God to heal her eyes. Her faith blessed me. She had been wearing contacts and glasses in an attempt to see better, and as soon as she asked me to pray for her sight, God touched her and she received perfect vision. She came back the next night to surrender her life to Christ. When she sent me a letter a few weeks later I learned her testimony. Not only had she been healed, but the Lord also had instantly delivered her from alcoholism.

No one, no matter how wonderful he or she may be, will ever be able to truly satisfy the longing only God can fill.

From that time on God opened the heavens over the meeting, and one by one people were receiving miracles. One child was brought in with bowlegs, and in front of the congregation God straightened out his legs. People with walking sticks were dancing freely, and the Holy Spirit was moving with power. One man got so excited that God had healed his chronic skin condition that he wanted to take his shirt off to show everyone his new skin. He was weeping as he tried to explain how terrible his skin condition had been.

Night after night went like this. God showed up; people got healed! On the last night, which I'll never forget, little baby Kayla was brought up to me. Kayla was a foster child, eighteen months old, and it was suspected that she had been shaken as an infant, causing her to have no control of her eyes, which seemed to float around of their own accord in different directions. As a result, she had no sense of balance and couldn't walk. As we prayed, people gathered to watch what God would do. I had my arms stretched out in front of me and clasped my hands together in front of her face. The power of God was all over me to heal, and at precisely that moment, I watched her eyes roll back into place. The people gasped as they watched God instantly correct her eyes. Another man gave his life to the Lord on the spot as he saw the miracle. And Kayla was walking within days.

Thinking about it now still brings joy to my heart—every single person the Lord touched, every life changed. But it wasn't always like this.

I came to know God personally when I was twelve years old through a glorious encounter with God in worship. I found myself frustrated, and I told Him it was really hard to worship someone I couldn't see and didn't know. "Help!" was the cry that came from my heart. And right then, I had an encounter that changed me forever. God opened up the eyes of my heart and allowed me to see Him. I knew in a deeply personal way that He was real! "Help!" has been my frequent prayer ever since.

The Holy Spirit is longing to help us in more ways than we understand. He wants to be our best friend. I'd longed for a best friend as a child and clung to every friendship in a way that was desperately codependent. You see, we are all created with a deep longing for connection with someone who will fulfill us and give us joy and purpose. Hollywood would like to tell us that we are longing for true love. It offers us the idea of a perfect human counterpart who will fill all our emotional and human needs. But the reality is that no one, no matter how wonderful he or she may be, will ever be able to truly satisfy the longing only God can fill.

You were made for fellowship with God Himself. In fact, He created humans to be His counterpart, His bride, the ones with whom He would have the closest connection. In the years I spent walking with God before I began ministering publicly, I discovered how much I really needed this relationship. He is my everything! And though I have been blessed with a beautiful family, nothing and no one compares to Him. As lovely as my husband and children are, they cannot come close to meeting my need for love and fellowship. I can talk with the Lord night and day, and He understands me and loves me completely.

Eighteen years after I came to Christ, God opened the doors for me to begin full-time ministry. But the years in between were not wasted years. God was at work preparing me, giving me hinds' feet to be able to stand safely on the high places of influence He had planned for me. It was in those years, some of them very difficult, that I learned the transforming power of perseverance. I found Him as my Lord, my vision, my best friend, and my strength. In the wilderness times I walked through, He helped me grow, teaching me about His nature and character. By His grace God showed me what was really important, shifting my focus away from myself, my problems, and my ministry and onto Him, His faithfulness, and His kingdom. And it was in the wilderness that I learned about the necessity of vision.

WITHOUT A VISION, PEOPLE PERISH IN THE WILDERNESS

Vision acts as a compass for us in the wilderness. When circumstances seem to be so contrary to the promises and hope is hard to find, we need vision. And the first and most foundational vision we need is of Him. We must know Him! In beholding Him, we are transformed into His image from glory to glory (2 Cor. 3:18). In finding Him as Lord, Savior, and friend, we find the fulfillment and security we long for. And knowing Him who is love empowers us to have faith to believe His faithful promises.

We can declare with confidence, "He who has purposed it will also do it" (see Isaiah 46:11).

God is faithful. In fact, His name "Faithful and True" is written on His robe. But in the wilderness, when we can't see how in the natural His promises could come to pass, it can be difficult to rest and be happy. We can be tempted to think, "When I find my spouse, when that one I love comes to Christ, or when I get my breakthrough, I will be happy." Yet sadly, if we delay being happy until a promise is fulfilled, we may never be happy. What happens when you get what you are praying for? Won't there be another thing to hope for? If you are believing for a spouse, won't you need other breakthroughs after you are married? There is always a need for faith as long as we live, and we need to learn how to be joyful at every stage of the journey. God wants us to be joyful in the wilderness, and that joy comes from communion with Him. In His presence is fullness of joy! Communing with God gives us reassuring confidence that He is in control, and peace that passes human understanding floods our hearts. Joy that goes beyond human sense is available when we make pursuing His presence our priority.

> *Vision acts as a compass for us in the wilderness.*

In those times when we are waiting for the fulfillment of a promise, it helps to get a picture of what God is saying. God did this for Abraham when He told him to go outside and look up at the stars. God asked Abraham if he could count them and then told him the stars were a picture of how many descendants he would have. He did the same when He asked Abraham to imagine counting the grains of sand on the seashore. God wants us to get a picture in our hearts of what His promises will look like. Are you believing for a loved one to be saved? Picture that person worshipping God. Imagine him or her passionate about the kingdom. These sorts of activities are not vain imaginations; they are using the gift of imagination God has given you to walk around in the promise of God and help you focus in the direction God is moving.

Like the spies who went into the Promised Land, you can walk around in your promise before you possess it and stir up your faith and joy about what God has given you. Your imagination is not evil. It is like a whiteboard that you, the Lord, or the enemy can write on. But it is yours to steward, and you have a choice as to what you entertain or view on your screen. We need to reject what is not pure and lovely and of a good report—anything that exalts itself above the truth of God's faithfulness—and replace it with what is true according to God's promise and will. What we focus on is what we will head toward, so we must be very aware of what has our attention.

I remember once waking up with stiff finger joints, and I began to worry that I might be getting arthritis like my mother had. As I was having this thought, I recognized that it was a trap from the enemy and immediately rejected the picture of illness. I deliberately began to imagine myself as a ninety-year-old lady with supple fingers, playing the piano and wearing my rings. The next morning my fingers were stiff again. Again the enemy tried to get me to imagine life with arthritis and to be fearful, but I chose to reject the thought and began to picture myself with beautiful, healthy, ninety-year-old joints. This went on for a week, until finally I had no more issues with my joints. Now, ten years later, I still have no pain or problems. There is great power in our thoughts, and we need to steward them to align with heaven's plans. What we focus on is what we will inherit.

The spies who were sent into the Promised Land were faced with similar tests. They went into the land promised by God and walked around in it, tasting the fruit and seeing its beauty. But they also saw giants in the land. Ten spies came back and reported on the giants because that is what they chose to focus on, while the other two, Joshua and Caleb, gave a glowing testimony of the goodness of the land and began telling the people God was well able to help them possess it. One group saw the good things but focused on the problem, while the others saw the problem but focused on the promise. As a result only Joshua and Caleb inherited the promise. As you fellowship with God and get to know Him in His goodness, His love will cause your faith to flourish, and the Holy Spirit will help you to focus on the promise, not the problem.

CHRIST IN YOU—THE BIRTHPLACE OF DREAMS

Christ, the hope of glory, lives within us by faith. So when we're in intimate communion with Him, His heart blends with our hearts, which become fertile ground for the seeds of His dreams to be planted, cultivated, and grown. He could just give us commands and force us to follow them, but that isn't the kind of relationship He wants to have with us. He wants such intimacy that our hearts sync with His and we live from our desires together.

This is not pie-in-the-sky dreaming. God allows us to dream in the hope that we will begin to walk around in His promises by faith before we have ever seen them in the natural. Heaven and earth are colliding, and God is bringing them together through the dreams He is putting in the hearts of His people.

In order for us to dream with God like this, He has to wake us up to the truth of our identity—that it is no longer we who live but Christ who lives in us (Gal. 2:20). It is actually He who is at work in us, both to will and to work for His good pleasure (Phil. 2:13). When we come to Him in intimacy and yield ourselves to Him and worship, things happen. Our hearts begin to beat with His. We see things He wants to do, and He extends an invitation for us to join Him in those things.

Now think about this: If that is what is going on inside of us—if we really believe that it is no longer we who live but Christ who lives in us—what should our lives look like? Scripture makes it clear: "As He is, so are we in this world" (1 John 4:17, NKJV). What is God like? The answer to that is your new identity and the truth you need to walk in. Doesn't Jesus want to have major influence? When you walk into a room, does He in you want to just be able to survive the atmosphere or blend in with it? Or has He destined you to change the atmosphere? Does He want you to live under the influence of the world or to become an influencer of it? Does the life you're living reflect the impact Jesus wants to have on you and those around you?

> *In order for us to dream with God, He has to wake us up to the truth of our identity.*

We have the light and life of Jesus, the hope of glory, within us, but I believe many have been tricked into hiding the light under a bushel. Many have been walking around with the covers of false humility or the fear man limiting their light. Some have battled with wrong religious thinking that has made them believe they have no right to dream big. We need to discover the truth of who we are. It's a deception that says, "I'm only human. I'm just giving it a go. I'll try my best." Does that really reflect who Jesus is? God says, "What are you doing? It's no longer you who live, but Christ who lives in you."

You have the power of God within you. You have His glory. You haven't been given a little bit of Jesus; you are in Him, and He is in you. God hasn't given you just one, two, or five talents, like the master gave his servants in Jesus's parable. He has blessed you with the greatest treasure of all—the Son of God Himself! You have been given His Spirit, His nature, His power, and His authority. If the servants were held to account and rewarded for what they did with what they were given, how much more do we need to be good stewards of the King of all kings, the Spirit of God's Son living in us? Hiding Him under a bushel and failing to dream big is a lot like someone burying his talent in the ground, and it doesn't please God.

Scripture says, "Arise, shine, for your light has come, and the glory of the LORD has risen upon you" (Isa. 60:1, MEV). We are responsible for stewarding the amazing privilege of having the Son of God in us and starting to dream accordingly. We have to deliberately wage war in our own minds and refuse to align our thoughts with anything other than the thoughts of Jesus. We have to declare what is already true of us—that we have the mind of Christ—and take every thought captive that exalts itself against who He is. That's a moment-by-moment choice that begins when we wake up in the morning and think about what we're going to do that day. We can't afford to float through life. God wants us to take captive not only every thought that is contrary to Christ, but also every thought that is contrary to Him *in us.*

So if any thought—including your perception of yourself—doesn't line up with the truth of Jesus in you, learn to reject it. When I wake up in the morning, I like to remind myself of what I look like. We all behold the glory of the Lord as in a mirror (2 Cor. 3:18), and as we look into the mirror of who He is, we see our reflection. We look like Him! In Christ, He is faithful to forgive me as I repent of my sin, so I can then by faith see myself righteous and pure. No matter what I may feel like, Scripture tells me that even if my heart condemns me, Christ is greater than my heart (1 John 3:20). So I remind myself that I am full of power by His Spirit. I am pure and righteous because of the blood of the Lamb. I am peaceful, kind, and patient. Everything the Bible says about love in 1 Corinthians 13 is now the reality of my nature because God is love, and it's not me living today but Him living in me. I begin to imagine how people will respond when they meet me. How will they be impacted when they encounter the peace and joy I have? The truth is that Jesus is peaceful and joyful today, so that's what is exuding out of me. Without looking into the mirror of what the Word says about Him, I get deceived into living a life dictated by my flesh and feelings. But as I reckon myself dead and Christ alive in me, I can start imagining what impact my life will have on others today.

I like to do this before I walk into a room, a function, a meeting, or even a family party. I check myself in the mirror of God's identity and think about deliberately releasing the atmosphere of heaven. I imagine how people are going to be impacted by His presence when they shake my hand. Instead of worrying whether I will be accepted or about how I look in the natural, I fix my thoughts on Christ in me and how He wants to minister to those I come in contact with.

> *If any thought—including your perception of yourself—doesn't line up with the truth of Jesus in you, learn to reject it.*

The hope of glory is in you. Your mission on earth is to be as He is in this world. When He speaks something to your heart, some thought or idea that glorifies Him and causes His kingdom to come on earth as it is in heaven, discipline yourself to recognize it and steward it. He has so many wonderful thoughts and ideas, and He shares them so generously. He will come and visit you with His dreams, inviting you into them. Don't dismiss them out of some false sense of humility. Don't cover up the glory of Jesus within you.

Once when I was praying for Australia some years ago, the Lord spoke to me. I had been asking God to send some rain on this thirsty land and bring revival. I had a vision of an underground sprinkler system, and the sprinklers were all connected. The sprinklers popped up and watered the nation. And as I prayed, I thought, "Oh, Lord, it would be so good if someone would pull the prophets together and we could get a relationship going. Someone should do that." And the Lord said, "What are you waiting for?" I suddenly realized this was a divine invitation. I wasn't supposed to just enjoy imagining how good it would be for someone else to do it. I had heard God correct me before for trying to give away opportunities He wanted to give to me. This was God wanting to do something. So as I spoke with those to whom I was accountable, the Lord confirmed what He was saying, and I was encouraged to step out and set up the Australian Prophetic Council. God continues to bless it with His favor today.

You see, God loves to put an idea in your heart about

doing something. And when He does, it's not just an idea; it's an invitation. The same thing happened with my first book, *Living in the Miraculous*. I procrastinated for so long. Prophetic people would come along and tell me I needed to finish, and I would agree with them. But I didn't really focus on it or make much progress. Cindy Jacobs came and prophesied that God had anointed me to write. And finally, after many promptings, I disciplined myself to make myself do it. When I did, many more doors began to open.

One problem many of us have with these divine invitations is that they may seem on the surface to be self-serving. I remember when God first spoke to me about recording a CD while I was still in Bible college. (In one of my wilderness seasons I had been writing songs that the Lord was giving me to help me trust Him and worship Him.) I was doing the dishes at the time, thinking that it would be good to put the songs He was giving me on a CD. I felt the Lord stirring in my heart the desire to do it. I said, "Oh, Lord, if that's You, if You really want me to do that, let the church call me and tell me that's what they want to do. Then I'll do it." I was afraid people would think I was promoting myself if I suggested it, so I put it off on them. As I was having this thought, I felt the Lord sternly rebuke me for shirking the responsibility to take the initiative He was trying to birth in me. Then I began to realize what I had said to Him. I was giving in to the fear of man and avoiding the responsibility to do anything about it. Little did I know how God wanted to use that project. After it was done, people wrote to me saying they had been delivered from suicidal thoughts as they had listened to the CD. Others wrote in to testify of being healed. The dreams God gives you are not just about you. There are people He wants to touch through you.

Some people have the same reservations I used to have

about this. I really didn't want to give the impression that I think a lot of myself, and I was quite worried people would get that idea if I voiced some of my dreams. But if you are so afraid of becoming proud—or being perceived that way—that you're afraid to dream, something is wrong. You can trust that God will humble you if you get too proud; He has plenty of ways, so don't worry about that. But most people have the opposite problem. They are so tentative that they won't dream of something glorious or make a decree about it. They limit themselves—and Jesus within them—out of fear and rob people of the blessings they would otherwise receive.

This fear is really a form of pride, if you think about it. It shows more concern for our own reputations than it does for the King of Glory within us. If the King of kings is in us, who are we not to think big? If we are going to steward God's presence, we are going to have to get used to His huge, glorious, audacious plans to touch the world. We have to begin to give our focus and attention to what the Spirit is saying and doing right now. I believe that when we do, we will be launched into some very exciting new things.

Now, I don't encourage rushing out and doing things without good counsel and wise advice. I'm not saying you should act on every whim you get. Test the words you receive to make sure they are from God, and remember that plans fail for lack of godly counsel. But if you're waiting on God to roll out the red carpet, hand you a microphone or an embossed invitation, and beg you to do what He is calling you to do, then you may be waiting a long time. He has asked you to be faithful with what He has given you. If God has spoken, the next move is yours. When Peter saw Jesus walking on the water, he recognized the desire that rose up in his heart to be with Jesus where

He was, doing what He was doing, as a divine invitation. Like Peter, you need to say, "Lord, if it's really you, tell me to come to you, walking on the water" (Matt. 14:28, NLT), and then be prepared to follow through!

> *If the King of kings is in us, who are we not to think big?*

I believe God is beginning to put iron in the backbones of believers—the courage to say yes to His thoughts and ideas. Trust His timing, of course, but if you will bring those dreams and desires to Him, asking for wisdom in the way to move forward, He will guide you into the next steps. Seek His direction, but seek it with a yes in your heart.

I once heard someone say that when he turned forty, God challenged him to write down a hundred dreams. Have you ever tried to do that? You may be able to write the first five or ten easily, but after that you really need to start to examine what is actually stored in your heart. I began to do that and encouraged my family to do the same. I began to make declarations like, "I see spina bifida healed in my meetings," and, "The lame walk and the blind see in my meetings without anyone even laying hands on them." Pretty soon, many of those declarations started coming to pass, and I needed to think of more! It began with a woman being healed of spina bifida, and then people started being healed before I could give the word of knowledge about their condition. I began just declaring what the Lord had done as the Lord showed me who was healed. I have begun to literally "live the dream," and God keeps challenging me to dream bigger. It is my responsibility to dream with God, because it's not about me. I have been crucified with Christ, and now He lives in me and wants to touch the world with His love through me. This is a truth every believer needs to recognize.

Those who know me have seen God do some pretty wild and exciting things for me as I've made declarations over what He says to me. A few years ago I was watching Sid Roth's show *It's Supernatural!* with my children and suddenly felt so strongly in my spirit that God would one day allow me to be on that show. I turned around and said to my children, "I'm going to be on *It's Supernatural!*" God must have put His angels to work when I said that. He sent prophets my way to help me through the process of writing my book and keep me going. He would sometimes speak to me to remind me I would be on television one day.

I would also make declarations that God was going to give me His favor with many media platforms, and I began declaring that I was going to be on TV all over the world, preaching even while I'm asleep. Why would I say such things if they hadn't happened yet? Because I learned to speak out whatever the Lord puts on my heart and then to patiently wait for Him to work it out as I follow whatever He says to do.

Eventually the dreams began to manifest. (It seemed sudden, but God sometimes spends years preparing one of His "suddenlies.") Years later I received an invitation to be interviewed on Sid Roth's show after my first book came out. Now we have begun producing our television program *Glory City TV*, and God is opening doors for it to be aired all over the world. I actually do share the gospel around the world while I am asleep! Don't forget what God promises, because if you will trust His faithfulness and patiently expect Him to do it, you will see it come to pass.

This is really a wonderful way to live. God has more for you than you've ever understood. He is giving you dreams—you've experienced His downloads into the desires of your heart, I'm sure—and He's waiting for you to add discipline to those dreams. He's giving you the opportunity to recognize what He's doing, speak it out, and process it with Him. "Lord, I've heard Your invitation. I want to talk about this with You. What do You want to do? What do You want to say? How do You want to do it, and what steps should I take?" Again and again, this process plays out in the lives of those who have the courage to believe that Jesus is in them working out His will.

KNOW THE SEASON AND STEP INTO IT

We are living in exciting times, and the excitement will only increase if we will step up and step over into a new place. God is doing glorious things, and many more are waiting for us. He is asking His people to say, "Yes, Lord, I will follow You. I am willing to give You my life—not just once and for all, but every moment of every day." He is calling disciples to leave their nets and follow Him, just as His first disciples did, and enter into a life of supernatural adventure.

If you can commit to follow Him this way, you will receive more dreams and desires from God. He will implant His heart into yours, and you will grow in your understanding and anticipation of the glorious works He is doing. God wants to expand your influence because He wants to be big for you and those in your realm of influence. He wants to be seen, and He wants the testimony of Jesus to go as far as it can possibly go. He wants people to interact with Him and know Him more deeply than ever. And He wants to use you as a vessel for these things. But it will require you to become more disciplined in your thinking. It isn't enough to have God's dreams; you have to steward them.

I strongly encourage you to tell the Lord, "Yes, God, I see what You are doing, and I want to partner with You.

I want to be like the disciples who left their nets and followed. I want my heart to meld with Yours, to beat with Yours, to share Your passions and desires. I want Your glory to cover the earth just as the waters cover the sea. And I want You to show Your glory through me as I cooperate with You and declare things that are not as though they already are and begin to walk in them."

If you look to Him, He will help you. You may feel as though the heavens are closed over your life, but the only way that can happen is if you close your eyes. In His light, you will see light. He will help you see if you will open your heart to Him. You can come before Him and look into His eyes, because it's in His light that He helps you see. Do you feel heavy? Tell Him. Discouraged? Ask Him to encourage you. Guilty or ashamed? Be honest with Him, and He will forgive and restore. There's nothing you can't bring to Him. God is waiting to engage in divine exchange with you. He wants to take your ashes and give you beauty. Bring Him your guilt and sin, and He will give you His righteousness. Give Him your grief, and He will give you joy. He'll take your confusion and give you peace. In fact, the Holy Spirit stands jealously by, waiting to help us in all our troubles, knowing that He has the answer and the help we need. We *have not* simply because we *ask not* (James 4:2)! Whatever is weighing you down, release it to God in faith, and He will give you whatever you need in its place. He is more willing to help you than you are to come to Him.

There is no condemnation for anyone who comes to God in faith, believing in His ability to forgive and transform. And His desire is to see His Son lifted up in you, to make His face shine on you, like a father lifting up his son and looking into his face with pure joy and delight. He is not worried about you assuming too much; He wants you to do even greater works than Jesus did. Why? Because that honors Jesus, the hope of glory who is in you, and it gives you complete joy, satisfaction, and fulfillment. He is so faithful to complete what He is doing in you. Simply lose sight of yourself and begin to think as He thinks.

What God is opening up to you right now—and to believers all over the world—is beautiful and marvelous. It's exciting. Step into it with boldness. Dream His dreams, pursue His desires, and enter with faith and confidence into the glorious days He has for you to experience.

Chapter 2

FINDING GOD IN THE PROCESS

I RECENTLY PICKED UP one of my old journals that I call my wilderness journal. It covers the late 1990s up to about 2001 and is filled with prayers, scriptures, little conversations with God, revelations, confessions of sin, and declarations of faith. During that season of life I had lots of promises from God and hardly any fulfillment in hand. But the visions and dreams were strong. As I reread this journal, I recalled the long process I went through to reach the time of fulfillment, and God began to show me some exciting things.

No one really likes to talk about process. It isn't a very popular topic. We live in an age of instant gratification, when microwaves and drive-thru windows give us what we want as soon as we want it. But you can't read about the great people of faith in the Bible without noticing that God spent years on them before bringing them into the place of promise. There was a process, and it was rarely an easy one. Many of them lifted up lots of prayers and cried plenty of tears before stepping into the fulfillment of God's calling. Process is part of God's plan.

It encourages me to know that most great men and women of God also went through many of the things we experience. Looking at the lives of people such as David and Joseph and the wilderness times they walked through, I saw how they were rejected by family members and those who should have helped them. They were over-looked, falsely accused, misunderstood, and mistreated. But after they came through, they were different. They had learned so much that would prove useful later, and they were stronger, having used the trials as opportunities to find God in intensely personal and powerful ways.

That's the theme of Psalm 84, which can be extremely encouraging if you're in a wilderness season:

> Blessed are those whose strength is in you, whose hearts are set on pilgrimage. As they pass through the Valley of Baka, they make it a place of springs; the autumn rains also cover it with pools. They go from strength to strength, till each appears before God in Zion.
>
> Hear my prayer, Lord God Almighty; listen to me, God of Jacob. Look on our shield, O God; look with favor on your anointed one.
>
> Better is one day in your courts than a thousand elsewhere; I would rather be a doorkeeper in the house of my God than dwell in the tents of the wicked. For the Lord God is a sun and shield; the Lord bestows favor and honor; no good thing does he withhold from those whose walk is blameless.
>
> —Psalm 84:5–11

This psalm talks about those who pass through the Valley of Baka, which literally means the "Valley of Tears." There is absolutely no condemnation in these verses for those who go through that valley; experiencing trouble in this world doesn't mean you've done something wrong. I used to think it did; I assumed God was punishing me for something if I was having a hard time. God may discipline us if we are stubbornly going off in a direction contrary to His will, but that's to bring us back, not to punish us. God is for us. More often our hardships have absolutely nothing to do with God's discipline. Jesus assured His disciples that there would be trouble in this world. It's a given. But He also assured them He had overcome the world (John 16:33). The Valley of Tears is a common experience, and overcoming it is meant to be a common experience too.

REDEFINING THE VALLEY

Did you notice what Psalm 84 says of those who go through the Valley of Tears? "They make it a place of springs." It's an extraordinary claim. There's fruitfulness in the valley experiences. Those who are able to look to God in hope and not get stuck in the frustration of the wilderness will eventually come out of it having produced fruit they didn't even know about. Somehow God makes the wilderness a vital preparation for the promise. You may have to go through a few wildernesses in order to get where He wants you to be.

> *Experiencing trouble in this world doesn't mean you've done something wrong.*

"Those who sow in tears shall reap with joyful shouting" (Ps. 126:5, NAS). There is always hope for those who are in Christ. He promises to make it all work for our good. But I believe we need to wage war with the promises of God in order to see them come to pass (1 Tim. 1:18). Faith is not passive; we must exercise it. Through faith and patience the heroes of Hebrews 11 inherited the promises, and we need to exercise that same faith. In the Valley of Tears, we can literally sow our pain and tears as seed that will bring forth a harvest of promises. I don't like to waste a drop of pain, because I know my tears are precious to God and that He longs for us to exchange them in faith for hope. For our former shame, pain, and disgrace,

Isaiah 61:7 promises us that God will give us double recompense, and in the Valley of Tears we have an opportunity to make a faith claim on this verse. On the days when it seems that all you have left is ashes and tears, take heart. Ashes, mourning, and heaviness are all currency that can be exchanged in prayer for God's beauty, praise, and joy.

I thank God now for the things He brought me through. I didn't necessarily thank Him as I was going through them. I really struggled. That's clear from what I wrote in my journal. I would write down what I was thinking, which usually involved some frustration. Then I would talk to God, listen for His answers, and write down what He said. It's basically a book of Katherine's psalms, beginning with a problem or concern and ending with hope, with a bit of struggle and lots of tears in between. And I can look back and see how He was releasing hope to me again and again in the midst of those experiences.

God will do that in our seasons of wilderness. I clung to His promises—things that, if you knew me then, you might have thought were wild imaginations that would never come to pass. But they *have* come to pass because God is faithful and true. I would talk to Him about these visions and dreams and about the despair I was feeling over them. And He would give a word of encouragement to keep me going and remind me how trustworthy He is.

GOD IS FOR YOU!

When God is for you, who can be against you? This is one of the most valuable things we can discover as we walk through difficult seasons. God is faithful and true and longs to comfort us in all our troubles. As God was preparing me to lead, He had me walk through a long season of serving in the place of hiddenness. Just as Joseph served in Potiphar's house in preparation for his role in Pharaoh's palace and David served in Saul's court in preparation for his role as king, we must serve in humility wherever God places us. And just as both of these men served until they were literally forced out, we need to learn what it is to love and be loyal to those who may not be the kindest of leaders. We need to learn that life is not about our promotion, but about His!

I grew up in church and served in just about every department. As a young person, I helped in children's church, conducted the children's choir, and served as a leader in the youth group. After Tom and I married, we moved to help build a new church that our youth pastor had started. I served on the worship team as a backup singer and an adult choir director, and I helped with home groups and women's ministry. Tom served as a deacon and elder. We were as involved as we could be.

When God first began to call me to preach, I was surprised. I had not seen many women in ministry, and though I knew of Kathryn Kuhlman's legacy and watched Joyce Meyer on TV, the only woman I had seen in the pulpit was the pastor's wife when she gave an annual Mother's Day message. I didn't even have a grid in my mind for a woman in leadership.

As an Australian married to a man of Finnish heritage, I was amazed by what I saw of Finnish housewives. They seemed to always have immaculately tidy houses and more home-baked food than anyone could ever eat. I tried for years to be a good Finnish housewife, and although my cooking was pretty average and my housekeeping skills were less than amazing, I enjoyed taking care of my family. I had no thought for anything more and didn't dream of doing anything ministry-related outside of singing on the worship team and maybe one day having the opportunity to lead worship.

At the age of twenty-three, I had an amazing encounter with God during a worship service in which the Lord delivered me and set me free from fear and rejection and the results of childhood abuse and abandonment. (See my book *Living in the Miraculous* for a full testimony.) Suddenly I began to have encounters at home and in church that really shook my paradigm. Some days I would groan and weep in intercession as I observed the sadness in the face of Jesus as He watched people blindly walk into eternity without Him. I had never seen a more tragic picture, and my heart broke for the Lord and His lost loved ones.

In prayer, I would have visions where I saw myself calling out to those who were blindly walking into a Christless eternity. I was often taken into visions where I would see fireballs rolling over crowds of people as I preached and sang. People were getting out of wheelchairs and being miraculously healed as the presence of God swept across auditoriums. I knew I was being called to preach, prophesy, heal the sick, and reach out to the lost and see them reconciled with this God who loved them more than life. I didn't know how it would happen, but I knew God was calling me.

I remember waking one morning to an open-eyed vision of a word being spelled out in front of me: G-A-L-I-A-H. I searched for the meaning but couldn't find it. But the word was seared into my memory, and I knew God was speaking. I thought maybe it was a clue to a Bible college I should attend or something important like that, but I didn't know where to look. We didn't have an Internet connection, and although I tried to find this word, it remained a mystery to me.

About three months later, I awoke to the same open-eyed vision, and by this time we had access to the web. My investigations led me to discover that this word was, in fact, a Hebrew female name that meant "wave" or "Wave of God." This really excited me, as I had also been having repeating dreams of a tsunami of miracles sweeping across my nation and the globe. Twentieth-century healing minister Smith Wigglesworth and contemporary prayer leader George Otis Jr. had both prophesied that the last great move of the Holy Spirit before the coming of the Lord Jesus would begin in Australia, New Zealand, and the islands of the South Pacific, and spread from there to all the nations of the earth. I knew the Lord was showing me that I was somehow destined to be an integral part of that great move.

My hunger to see people saved and the sick healed seemed to grow every day as I became desperate to see God move. I remember weeping as I watched videos of the late evangelist Kathryn Kuhlman and heard the testimonies of healing, and I would cry out in prayer for God to use me as He had used her. My journal documents my desire and request for the gift of healing. My hunger led me to cry out for a baptism of fire and to study everything I could find on the healing revivalists of old. I remember the day I first read an extract from Maria Woodworth-Etter's *A Diary of Signs and Wonders*. I had to go and cry, as she seemed to articulate the very things that were on my heart.

I went to my pastor and tried to explain what was going on, and he suggested I enroll in Bible college. So I did that with great fervor and did very well. However, I struggled with some of the theology, particularly with regard to the will of God for healing. I was so passionate about truth that on some days I would go home and cry for hours after hearing a message suggesting God wanted to heal people only occasionally and that more often than not sickness and injury were meant to teach us something. From my study of the Word and from the writings of all the healing revivalists I had researched, I was convinced that Jesus healed everyone, without exception, who came to Him for healing. He is the same yesterday, today, and forever, and if we don't build our theology on who Christ the rock is, we are on sinking sand. To suggest anything else was like a red rag to a bull for me because I knew that without a solid belief in the will of God to heal, I would always have doubt in my mind when it came to praying for the sick. I knew God was good and wanted to heal all our diseases and that by His stripes we were healed. We could trust that it was His will to heal. So when it came my turn to preach in the Bible college chapel meeting, I was prepared with a good message to tell them the truth and correct all their wrong thinking. I was ready to sock it to them!

The night before chapel, though, the Holy Spirit started speaking to my heart. Gently He showed me that I didn't really have love or compassion for the people to whom I was going to speak. I needed to learn the difference between loving to speak the truth and speaking the truth in love. Without love we are just a clanging gong and an annoying sound! I felt the Holy Spirit ask me to preach on God's love instead. I had passion and fire in my belly, but I needed a revelation of love, and I needed to be known by my love for others before I could try to correct them. The prophet in me loves truth, but we must love people rather than just being in love with our own opinions.

Embrace God's correction, and you will grow. Reject it, and you will continue to go around the mountain until you have learned the lesson you need in order to be promoted. If I can offer any advice to those in this place of process, it would be this: surrender quickly to God's correction, and you will save yourself some pain. God is far more patient than we are and will persevere in teaching us His ways. I had cried out for fire but didn't realize that God also used fire to release us from all that is contrary to His nature.

Jacob went through this process. God wrestled with him all night, trying to bring him to the place of surrender, until finally He touched Jacob's hip so he would acknowledge his weakness. Jacob refused to let Him go, knowing that he needed God's blessing (Gen. 32:22–32). The Father's heart for us is that we would desire to be with Him. On the road to Emmaus, Jesus appeared as though He would keep walking; only after the traveling disciples prevailed upon Him to stay did He open their eyes to recognize Him (Luke 24:13–35). God wants us to want Him.

> *Without love we are just a clanging gong and an annoying sound!*

But as Jacob wrestled with God, it wasn't until he acknowledged that he was Jacob the supplanter that he was transformed and given a new identity. God renamed him "Israel," one meaning of which is "prince of God." We have the opportunity in our times of struggle to humble ourselves and learn how much we need Him. As we demonstrate our desire for His fellowship and presence, just as Moses did in the wilderness when he said he would not go unless God's presence went with him, we begin to build real friendship with God. And when we learn how to surrender whatever dross God may be after, we discover the truth that in yielding we become victorious.

One of the visions God gave me during a wilderness season was of a car being put up on a rack, as if it were being prepared for service work underneath. I didn't like the look of that; it meant God was going to make some adjustments. I saw another vision of God inviting me on a walk that led off into a garden, but it wasn't the way I wanted to go because I was so focused on what I wanted to do that a walk in a garden seemed like a waste of time. I would go into these experiences kicking and screaming, certain I was being punished for something. But the truth of these visions was that God had seen the yes in my heart in response to His call. I wanted to know Him more. And in order to give me that knowledge of Him, He allowed me to walk through things that, though sometimes painful, provided some clarity.

He does that often, taking us to a place of new perspective before we take new ground. The dealings of God are really often the beginning of God answering our prayers and giving us the longings of our heart, even though it may not feel like it at the time. It's what we would really want if we knew where the process was taking us. Life is not always easy. But when you find yourself going through difficult things, you have a choice: you can come out having just survived, or you can come out leaning on the arm of your Beloved. You can experience the tears and nothing more, or you can go through the Valley of Tears and make it a place of springs. You'll get through either way, but how you respond determines your experience as you come out.

> *When we learn how to surrender whatever dross God may be after, we discover the truth that in yielding we become victorious.*

I strongly encourage you to spend some time in Psalm 84. It's a key passage for those going through the wilderness. It says, "Blessed are those whose strength is in you, whose hearts are set on pilgrimage" (v. 5). In other words, those who have said, "Lord, You're all I want! You're all

I'll ever need!" are blessed and favored because they have found their strength in God rather than in their circumstances. Those who are deliberate in choosing God as their highest, deepest desire will be made happy. Wherever the path leads, whether it's through a valley of weeping or through joyful mountaintop experiences, they will find hope in Him, and that hope will not disappoint.

We also see this promise in Isaiah 43:

> Do not fear, for I have redeemed you; I have called you by your name; you are Mine. When you pass through waters, I will be with you. And through the rivers, they shall not overflow you. When you walk through the fire, you shall not be burned, nor shall the flame kindle on you. For I am the LORD your God, the Holy One of Israel, your Savior.
> —ISAIAH 43:1–3, MEV

God says that no matter what you walk through, He will be with you. You will not be a victim in your experiences; you'll be a victor. In your weakness, you will discover supernatural strength. Your faith will be tested but will come forth as gold. You will go from strength to strength because you will find Him wherever you turn. These are experiences that will set you up for the rest of your life because you will personally know who God wants to be for you. That experiential knowledge can never be taken away. And you can only learn it in the wilderness.

A PLACE OF SINGING

Joseph went through a long process. He had a dream about being in a position of influence and authority with his brothers bowing down to him. That didn't make them very happy, so they ambushed him and sold him into slavery. Years passed as Joseph suffered first as a slave and then as a falsely convicted prisoner. He was molded and trained as he served under a slave master.

> *Those who are deliberate in choosing*
> *God as their highest, deepest*
> *desire will be made happy.*

He was tested regarding his use of power when he was appointed Potiphar's second in charge. He was tested regarding his level of purity when Potiphar's wife tried to draw him into an illicit relationship, and he was tested regarding his level of integrity in prison. Every time it looked as if he had reached the lowest possible point, he was taken even lower. He could have given up in despair, but he didn't. Psalm 105:19 tells us that until the word of the Lord came to pass, it tested Joseph. It stretched him. It forced him to choose whether to believe against all visible evidence or to give in and give up. As Joseph was tested, he let God's promise become like iron in his soul.

Most of us who have been through a wilderness or are currently going through one can relate to that. When God has said one thing and circumstances contradict it, you are tested in many ways, sometimes almost to the point of despair. It's an extreme stretching. I look back at my wilderness journals and wish I could go back in time to encourage myself, to say, "Keep going; it's going to get very good!" I wish I could have seen the end of the story then as clearly as I do now. But I realize in rereading my own words that I found an intimacy with God during those times that is so precious I would not want to have missed it. I learned keys to overcoming through those experiences. And I would not have gotten them if life had been rosy all the time. I found God when no one else understood me, and I discovered a joy that no one could ever take from me. I found in those times an intimacy with God that made my heart sing.

I didn't always feel like singing. There were times when I'd get discouraged and weep instead. In those times, I would deliberately write encouraging words to myself, reminding myself that God is faithful. I would decide to sing no matter what. I was like the barren woman in Isaiah 54, whom the prophet instructs to sing despite the fact that she's never had a child. If a barren woman could rejoice simply because of what God was going to do, so could I. If she could enlarge her tent, strengthen its stakes, and lengthen its cords before any descendants were visible, so could I. Why? Because the Maker Himself was her husband—and mine. He is the God of all the earth. He is powerful in any situation, even when the situation doesn't seem to change. And He is our best friend, the one who understands us completely and loves us unconditionally.

When we go through times of not understanding why life is unfolding the way it is, God is looking for us to fix our eyes on Him. Instead of getting into all the "when" and "why" questions, which can just torment us in our place of limited understanding, He wants us to take captive every thought against the knowledge of who He truly is. He is always the answer in every situation, and He will manifest Himself as the answer. Never once does someone approach God in Scripture—either the Father in heaven or Jesus on earth—and hear Him say, "Oh, that's so awful. Too bad for you. Just be brave and suffer through it." No, He always comes through with hope, deliverance, healing, power, and more. And He is the same today as He was then. He doesn't change.

That's why Psalm 84 says those who trust in Him are blessed. It isn't those who give in to frustration and despair who are blessed; it's those who continue to trust.

David said he would have lost hope if he had not believed he would see God's goodness in the land of the living (Ps. 27:13, NKJV). He fixed his eyes on the God who does not defer all promises to a future age but who comes through in our lifetime.

I did a lot of study on David's life during my wilderness time. God had given him amazing promises, but he was badly treated. He had been designated the next king, but the current king kept throwing spears at him until he was finally forced to flee for his life. He was maligned and hunted for years. He hid out in the wilderness and in enemy territory. In his worst moment, which we'll look at more closely later, his own men wanted to stone him. That meant everyone was against him—his family, the king, the nation, even his own faithful friends. Yet in that moment, he strengthened himself in the Lord. He found a supernatural strength to sustain him. Over all those years of exile, God transformed a shepherd boy into a mighty man after His own heart.

As David went through difficult and dry seasons, he found God and held on to hope. His dependence on God grew deeper and deeper roots. The building of character we experience in similar seasons is not very popular to talk about, but it's essential.

To come to the place where you realize that God alone is able to understand and help you through is the beginning of turning the valley into a place of springs. It may seem unjust that family, friends, or leaders are against you. But if you maintain integrity, faithfulness, and honor as David did in the face of the injustice, you will find the power that comes from leaning on God alone. He alone is unfailing and faithful, and He is the only one on whom we can totally rely.

Rejection tests us with the question, "Do you love me

more than these?" Peter was asked this question (John 21:15–17), and as he came to the revelation that in his own strength he was weak, God was then able to be strong for him. Perseverance in this sort of fire is worth it, for in the end, God will bring you forth as gold refined in the fire. Leaning on God is the posture for a new season.

When we're born again, we become new creations in Christ. We have the power to live for God and be free from sin. But we have to grow in grace and mature, and the only way to do that is to continually choose to know and follow God. Choosing Him is most meaningful when doing so goes against the waves of adversity. The wilderness grows us up.

Again, I'm not saying God orchestrates trouble. His plans are to prosper you and not to harm you, to give you a hope and a future (Jer. 29:11). But you will face trouble in this world, and you are not to be its victim. You never have reason to say, "Woe is me; life's not fair." You always have a reason to resolve to hope in God and take heart. He has already overcome the world (John 16:33), so you already have a song to sing.

I wrote many songs in my valley of weeping. I wrote one titled "Faithful" when my dreams weren't even close to being realized. I wasn't involved in any form of ministry and was discouraged about a number of things. But I intentionally chose not to write songs about my discouragement. Instead I wrote about His faithfulness: "Lord, You're faithful. Everything I'll ever need, Your grace will lead me to. My hopes, my dreams, my destiny, my life is found in You. You are faithful; You are faithful; You are faithful."[1]

I would dig into Psalm 91 and ask Him to cover me with the feathers of His wings: "Bring me near and I'll come in close to You. Give me eyes that only look to You. Lift my head and help me see the lover of my soul who paid the price so I can now draw near. Cover me with the feathers of Your wings; cover me and draw me to Your side. Cover me that I might know the fullness of Your love and rest beneath the shadow of Your wings."[2]

As I began to cry out to God in song, deliberately declaring His faithfulness and thanking Him for being my comfort, my glory, and the lifter of my head, hope was stirred up. I was able to rest in Him. I knew He would be faithful and true.

Unique Opportunities in the Valley

As I go back and read my journals, I realize what a precious time the wilderness was. It was a time when God allowed me to really get to know Him. If you're going through a season when you haven't yet seen the fulfillment of promises God has given you, count on the fact that He has a plan, and it isn't just for you to endure pain. It's for you to turn the place of weeping into a place of springs. That is His plan for you, at least for now. It's really a unique opportunity; you will never have that chance when things are going well, and you'll never have it for all eternity in heaven. Now is the only time you can turn a valley into a mountaintop experience.

Turning the place of weeping into a place of springs is very simple, but it isn't always easy. You'll be tempted to slip into discouragement and despair at times. That's normal, and there is no condemnation from God for that. Temptation does not define you. But with every temptation, God provides a way of escape. He points you to a spring where you can go and drink deeply from the river of His presence. He has joy for you in that place, a peace that passes understanding. And if you can find it there, you can have it forever. It won't come and go; you've already proven it can be constant. You've grabbed hold of it in the hardest of times. Nothing can take it from you. The giants of adversity become bread for you in that place.

> *You have to fix your eyes on something greater than what you're going through.*

The wilderness is part of the pilgrimage, but we are created for joy, even in the midst of that season. When you meet people who say, "I'm going through a wilderness," and you can tell they are in a place of misery, it isn't very encouraging, is it? You don't really want to be around them very much. That's because God didn't call anyone to simply survive. He called us to thrive. With His help, you can lay hold of supernatural strength and rejoice in all circumstances. And in the midst of your journey through the valleys, you can see incredible, glorious manifestations of God, because that's where you find Him. You discover the joy of intimacy with Him going through the valleys. Knowing Him causes the supernatural to flow.

That's why I hesitate to talk of wilderness and wonders as two different seasons of life. There are wonders in the wilderness too. They may be different kinds of wonders than the ones you're dreaming about, but they are just as miraculous and meaningful. Your encounters with God in those times become a foundation for all future experiences with Him.

In my journal I wrote out declarations of things I was believing for. Many of those things have now come to pass. That encourages me to write more declarations. The process works! If you can see something in the Spirit that is part of God's plan for you, you can have it. And if you're going through a wilderness season, you have to develop God's perspective. You have to fix your eyes on something greater than what you're going through because if you can see only your circumstances, life is going to feel pretty bleak. What you focus on is what you move toward.

Abraham kept his eyes on the promise. So did the all the heroes of faith mentioned in Hebrews 11. They had their sights set on a city they hadn't yet seen (Heb. 11:13–16). They were looking forward to the promises of God, even though some of those promises extended beyond their own lifetimes. They knew the power of vision.

THE SEASON OF THE SEER

I believe we are living in the season of the seer. God is encouraging you to look up and see, to begin to imagine all He has promised you, and in your heart to walk around in His promises and see them with eyes of faith. Begin to see yourself as He has seen you and declared you to be. Begin to see the promises He has put in front of you with the eyes of your sanctified imagination and the good works He has stored up in advance for you to do.

When you can see those promises, resolve not to lose your way. Keep your eyes focused on the one who can bring you safely to their fulfillment. The Israelites wandered in the desert because they lost their way. They looked at the Promised Land only with eyes of doubt, not with eyes of faith. Taking the land seemed too difficult. The giants were too big, and their unbelief caused them to miss out on God's promise.

Don't waste your wildernesses like that. This is your great opportunity to prepare for everything God has in store for your future. It's the perfect place to refine your vision and fix your eyes on truth. He wants you to find Him in the middle of your circumstances, not after you get out of them. He wants you to know Him like you've never known Him before and to discover His joy like you've never experienced it—to know His strength in your weakness. Let Him lift up your head, and see the plans He has for your future.

If you don't yet have a vision for the future, you are at risk of wandering aimlessly. What are the desires God has put in your heart? Write them down, no matter how wild they may seem. If fulfilling them is not beyond your natural ability, then it doesn't require faith. God wants to do more than you can hope and imagine!

If you do have a vision but haven't started writing it down, speaking it out in faith and making it plain, it's time to do so. God has a purpose and a plan for you, whether you know the specifics or not. Begin with what you do know. Submit your vision to God and let Him grow it. Then believe what you see and declare it.

I didn't know exactly how they were going to happen, but I began declaring the things God revealed to my heart, even though it took a while for me to believe what He was showing me. I thought perhaps what I was seeing was simply my wild imagination. So I prayed for God to tell my husband, Tom, about His plans for me and confirm them through him. (It was very uncommon for women to be in ministry in our church at the time, so I really wanted God to speak to my husband.) One day soon after, as we were driving in the car, Tom said to me, "I reckon you might make a good preacher." That's all he said, but I knew God was answering my prayer.

Still, Tom's comment wasn't enough for me. I asked God to send prophets to confirm my calling. I wanted the senior pastor to be in the room when a prophet spoke the calling over me so he could believe it too and help me get where I was going. I had it all figured out. If there were witnesses like that, I wouldn't be able to chalk the experience up to my own passions. And surely God would help me out since

He was willing to lead the Israelites with a pillar of fire by night and a cloud by day. So I asked God to set that up.

It didn't happen that way. Prophets would come and prophesy over others, and I'd get frustrated I wasn't picked. One told me, "Trust God, sister," and then moved on to the next person. I didn't understand why God didn't speak to him about me, and I sobbed my heart out about it. I told God if He didn't give me a prophetic word to confirm my calling the next time a prophet visited, I'd give the whole idea up. The next time the same thing happened again—a prophet said, "Trust God, sister," and kept moving. I was devastated. I couldn't seem to get the word I was looking for. One person saw me upset and prophesied that I just needed a long vacation. I went home upset, threw myself on the bed, and demanded that God speak to me.

Thankfully, He did speak to me, and it didn't come the way I expected. I was reading the story of Simeon in the Gospel of Luke, where the Spirit had revealed to Simeon's heart that he would see the Messiah before he died (Luke 2:25–35). The Spirit led him into the temple courts, and there he saw Jesus. Suddenly I saw it. Nobody had prophesied to Simeon; the Spirit revealed, and he believed. That was all. I felt such sorrow in my heart for not trusting the Holy Spirit like that. Right there I knelt down and repented for not believing the Holy Spirit had spoken to my heart. Out loud in my bedroom I declared, somewhat awkwardly, that even if no one ever prophesied it to me, I believed God was calling me to preach the gospel, heal the sick, and go to nations—on no other witness than the one God had put in my heart.

God wants us to trust Him in what He reveals to us. It's wonderful when He sends others along to help pull us out of the pit, but we have to be able to recognize a promise, know it's ours, and go after it, fixing our eyes only on the one who is faithful and true. We have to line our words up with what He is saying and agree that it will be done.

I believe God is giving each of us an opportunity in every moment to be aware of something that hasn't yet come to pass. We have an opportunity to simply survive or to allow our wildernesses to bring forth gold in our lives. As we allow God to bring forth faith like gold, we'll come out with much more power and peace. Even though His process seems slow at times, our faith can accelerate the process and catapult us much further than if we had merely struggled through. The valley really can be a place of springs, refreshing and beautiful and full of joy, no matter what the circumstances look like.

"I know the plans I have for you," says the Lord (Jer. 29:11). Surely He smiles when He looks at your future. You can fall back into His arms and tell Him, "Lord, my trust is in You. I'm not going to be a victim; I'm going to rest in hope because Your arms are strong. I'm going to come out of this leaning on my Beloved. My face will shine so brightly with Your radiance that people will want what I have."

"Fear not," says the Lord, "for I am with you" (Isa. 41:10, NKJV). Though you walk through the fire, you will not be burned. Though you pass through the waters, you will not drown (Isa. 43:2). He knows what you're walking through, and He wants you to fix your eyes on Him. He is releasing hope. It's all for your good. But you need to hone your vision.

A New Perspective

If you were driving and suddenly saw that the bridge over a giant chasm was out, would you just turn around and go another way? Or would you stop the car, forget everything you had scheduled, and try to warn people of the danger ahead? It's easy to get so caught up in your own dreams and in getting through the wilderness that you forget the reality of what a believer's ministry really is. We are all called to love God and love people. An inward focus makes us lose sight of the big picture—that without God, people are headed for grave danger and have no hope unless someone warns them and leads them to the Savior. We must love God enough to share the burdens of His heart and love people enough to reach out to them. Without this awareness, we are living blind to our true purpose.

In reading my old journals, I can see how focused I was on my own ministry aspirations. Fear makes us selfish, and selfish ambition is a symptom of not trusting in God's ability to fulfill His purposes. The Spirit has used my own words from the past to give me a fresh perspective and energy even now. Over the years, by His grace, He has taken me from being somebody who was concerned about my ministry to somebody who is concerned about God's heart and about people. In turning my focus to Him in that wilderness season, I began to get an eternal perspective. When we love God we will begin to love what He loves, and He takes it personally when we reach out to the lost. As much as we have done it to the least of these, God says, we have done it to Him (Matt. 25:40). If we lose sight of the Father's heart for the lost, we lose our way and miss out on the joy of bringing to God what blesses Him most: children reconciled to Him. Loving people really connects us with the heartbeat of God. He wants us to be able to see things from His perspective.

We learn things in the wilderness that we can't learn any other time.

God gives you a fresh perspective in your places of pain. You learn to focus on what's important. God draws you out of yourself and into Him, that place of true freedom. He shows you that He loves you more than life. He wants to hold you, comfort you, and walk with you. He trains you to see beyond yourself and into the vision of your true calling.

When God shows you that His ways are better than yours, give up on your own schemes. Don't go kicking and screaming. Just let go. It's a whole lot easier and more joyful when you come to believe that the wilderness isn't something God is *putting* you through. It's something He's *bringing* you through. That's different, isn't it? One is a burden; the other is a glorious victory. And it's all about your perspective.

That is a perspective learned best in the valley of weeping. It becomes a place of springs if we turn our focus to God and develop intimacy with Him. We learn things in the wilderness that we can't learn any other time, and we develop a hope that cannot be shaken and a joy that can never be taken away. And that joy—our delight in the Lord Himself—prepares us to bear the glory of the wonders that are coming.

Chapter 3

THRIVING IN THE
WILDERNESS

ANY OF THE things I dreamed about twenty years ago are now happening, and it's wonderful. As Proverbs 13:12 says, "A dream fulfilled is a tree of life" (NLT). But the joy of satisfied longings is ordinary compared to the joy I receive when I am alone with God. Some people think, "Lord, one day when I have a wife/husband I'll be happy," or, "Lord, I'll be really fulfilled when I get an invitation to preach in stadiums." They are waiting for their experience in order to have their joy.

These are good dreams, and it will be amazing when God fulfills them. But the joy and sense of fulfillment from those desires will not even come close to the fullness of joy God wants to release in your heart moment by moment in the process of getting there. He wants you to be happy now—in Him—even as you're waiting in the wilderness for the other things He has in store for you. Otherwise, God's joy would be available only at certain times of life, and we would go through long seasons without any sense of fulfillment.

The heart set on Him, no matter how many other desires it has, can be satisfied at any time. There is a deeper joy than seeing your dreams come to pass, a deeper joy than knowing God's promises and having them fulfilled. It's the deep, satisfying joy of knowing Him intimately in any season. Nothing can satisfy as He does.

Knowing and experiencing the truth that only God Himself truly satisfies is essential because as God imparts dreams to us and gives us His promises, and then we seek Him, declare the promises, and wait for their fulfillment, we will go through a wilderness. That's almost always the pattern in Scripture, and it's still true for anyone who receives His word by faith. There is often time between promise and fulfillment, and how we respond during that time often determines what we experience. The problem is that the journey can seem so dark at times, so hopeless and discouraging, that it's easy for us to lose sight of who God wants to be. Our wanderings are often worrisome experiences. But they don't have to be. Look at these two passages from the Book of Psalms:

> Let our dark night end and the sunrise of your love break through our clouded dawn again. Only you can satisfy our hearts, filling us with songs of joy and gladness to the ends of our days. Come and restore us.
>
> —PSALM 90:14, TPT

> One thing I desire; this shall I seek, that I may dwell in the house of the Lord all the days of my life to gaze on his beauty. Only you can satisfy.
>
> —PSALM 27:4, TPT

Do you see the common theme in these two verses? Only God can satisfy. I wrote a song about that during one of my wilderness seasons. "Only You can satisfy my soul" was my cry.[1] That's reality. The fulfillment of your dreams is not enough. Your goals and accomplishments are not enough. Your vision may help sustain you in the wilderness, but it won't be enough to fulfill you. Only He can satisfy you in the dry and barren moments of your life.

The Gateway to Wonders

The wilderness is part of our pilgrimage, but God never called anyone to just survive the wilderness. He trains us to thrive in it. God has given us a way to have supernatural joy beyond our understanding. If we can find that joy while we are still in the wilderness, we will walk through a gateway into a life of wonders.

The heart set on Him, no matter how many other desires it has, can be satisfied at any time.

Paul and Silas inspire me. On their first visit to Philippi, they were beaten and thrown into prison, where instead of lamenting their crisis they sang hymns of praise to God. The Lord sent an earthquake and broke them free, saving a prison warden and his family in the process. That was in the early days of the church in that city. But much later Paul wrote from another prison—this time while under house arrest in Rome, where he was awaiting a trial that could have determined whether he lived or died.

Paul had plenty of opportunities in that situation to see things negatively. He could have lamented his circumstances, attempted to bind the enemy and loose his chains, wondered if God had forsaken him, and written letters of complaint to believers outside the prison walls such as the Philippians.

Instead, he said his imprisonment was actually working out for good, as many in the Roman ranks were hearing the gospel. He wrote that even if others were preaching out of envy and strife and defaming his reputation, at least Christ was being preached, and that was worthy of celebration. And whether he lived or died? Well, either way was a victory. To die would be gain, as that would mean he would be with Christ in glory. To live meant more fruit-fulness among people such as the Philippians, as he could go on teaching and ministering. In every situation—none of which we would want for ourselves—Paul was seeing the positive.

When we get over to chapter 4 of his letter to the Philippians, we discover Paul's secrets for thriving in the wilderness. "Rejoice in the Lord always. Again I will say, rejoice!" (Phil. 4:4, MEV). Many of us have memorized this scripture; some can recall singing it enthusiastically in Sunday school. But God doesn't want us just to have it in our minds; He wants us to have it in our hearts—fully activated. It's a precious truth that we can rejoice in every situation, no matter what it looks like.

Rejoicing is God's way out of prison. It releases us from bondage. If you begin to rejoice in the midst of a storm, you're free. Praise is a weapon of warfare, and it is power-fully effective. When you rejoice and celebrate in all cir-cumstances, you overcome them.

Many people are under the false impression that if they don't bother the devil, he won't bother them. So they shrink back from getting involved in too much ministry because they want to avoid attack. If you've ever thought that, I have news for you: he's going to attack you anyway. And if you can stay really close to the one who protects you, you are in the best position. The enemy attacks through deception, and that only works with people who aren't in the light. If you're living in and focused on the light, you aren't really swayed by what goes on in the darkness. You can trust that God is working everything out for your good and then go ahead and rejoice in it.

Paul's next key for thriving in the wilderness involves prayer—but not just any prayer. It's prayer with a cer-tain attitude. "Be anxious for nothing, but in everything by prayer and supplication, with thanksgiving, let your requests be made known to God" (Phil. 4:6, NKJV). We often hope God will do something in answer to our desires without ever actually asking Him to do it. We let our longings, even little ones, turn into wishes rather than prayers. Every one of us has an intercessory instinct that was given by the Spirit. It's that impulse that says, "Oh, it would be so good if something good happened for that family." Or, "I do hope she gets her healing soon." That's an intercessory burden, and you'll carry it because you have God's heart. You care. But when you let those begin to pile up without taking them to God, they can really weigh on your heart. Like the old hymn says:

> What a friend we have in Jesus,
> All our sins and griefs to bear!
> What a privilege to carry
> Everything thing to God in prayer!
> O what peace we often forfeit,
> O what needless pain we bear,
> All because we do not carry
> Everything to God in prayer.[2]

God says He is looking for us to ask—not to be anxious about anything but to ask for His intervention with faith-filled confidence; not to pray with such tension and worry that it's less of a prayer and more of a pleading or a complaint, but to simply lift up our requests and anything weighing on our hearts with thanksgiving and without anxiety. Our prayers don't have to be long, but there's no reason we can't turn every compassionate impulse into a moment of intercession. And when we do that with gratitude for what God is going to do—knowing it will be good, whatever it is—then we bring breakthrough into that situation.

God is looking for us to become a praying people, even when we're in a wilderness and very aware of our own pain and needs. It is so hard to see the purposes of God and other people when we have our eyes focused on ourselves and our situations. The Holy Spirit wants to turn our focus outward so we can see the people around us who need His touch. I used to tell people I would pray for them, and then two weeks later I'd be kicking myself for forgetting. Now I just go ahead and pray on the spot. And I pray with faith and excitement in my heart because I know God hears and is already working. We can't pray, "Please, God, do something. Why haven't You done anything yet? Please!" That's an anxious prayer. Go ahead and thank Him instead. Without thanksgiving, it becomes just a worry. God is looking for us to make our requests known to Him in great expectancy and with gratitude for the answer He is already setting up.

When we do this, we can live with a clutter-free mind and heart. "And the peace of God, which surpasses all understanding, will protect your hearts and minds through Christ Jesus" (Phil. 4:7, MEV). God wants His peace to guard us. He doesn't want the people in our lives to become added burdens that weigh us down with concern. Compassion isn't heavy if we turn it into hopeful, grateful, confident prayers. He wants us to live clear and free. And we can if we rejoice always, pray about everything with thanksgiving, and let His peace rule within us. Then we can be like Jesus in the world, living as an opportunity for others to connect with God because of the light and life within us.

I remember praying for my daughter late one night. She had been away from God for several years, and it was a source of deep grief for me. Half an hour after I started to pray, she called to tell me a remarkable story. She had just come out of a function and was headed to her friend's car when some people drove by. This couple from my church were on a prayer drive, and the Holy Spirit asked them to stop and talk to my daughter, whom they didn't know or recognize. Because it was late at night they were concerned they might scare her, so they hesitated and kept driving. But the Holy Spirit persisted and they turned around.

By this time my daughter and her friend had driven to another spot to do their makeup before heading out for dinner. So the couple asked the Lord where they were, and the Holy Spirit directed them to where the girls had parked. They approached the car, reassuring the girls that they were Christians and that the Lord just wanted to speak to them. They began to prophesy over the girls with accurate words of knowledge. My daughter was amazed but told her friend that she knew about this type of ministry and assured her it really was God. Then she asked the young couple what church they came from. When they told her they were from Glory City Church (GCC), Jessica laughed and told them she is my daughter. (I am the senior pastor at GCC.)

After they left she called me, excited about what had happened. Although it was still some time before Jessica came back to the Lord and to church, this experience was key in helping her to come home. And it all happened while I was praying. Whatever your heart's cry is, ask and keep on asking, because God will do whatever we ask for according to His will when we ask in faith.

> *Put away anxious thoughts and choose to keep on rejoicing.*

God is extremely satisfying in this place. I believe that in this season of awakening, He's asking us to recognize these truths and apply them. He is giving us power to be fully aware and fully awake, alert, sober, and vigilant because the enemy is prowling around like a roaring lion looking for people to devour (1 Pet. 5:8). The enemy wants to crowd your heart with burdens and concerns and disappointments. He's afraid of you because you're part of God's plan to cover the earth with His glory as the waters cover the sea. God is looking to free you up, satisfy your soul, and fill you with joy. He wants you to arise and shine and fill the earth with His praise.

So God gives us ways of escape through rejoicing in Him, telling Him whatever is bothering us, gratefully and confidently asking Him to deal with it, and then resting in His peace. When the air gets clear, you can start to hear what He wants to say and come into agreement with it. You can enjoy being in a really sweet fellowship with Him. And then whoever you meet will get to experience the radiance of God in you.

God has created you to be a walking joy factory, a shining example of His peace, so you can make your face shine on everyone you meet. You can actually provoke others to joy simply by being who you are in Him. You're a gift. Put away anxious thoughts and choose to keep on rejoicing. And then rejoice some more. Pray, thank God for the answer, and fill your mouth with praise. Great wonders begin to happen in that place of worship and freedom.

BEYOND A WILDERNESS OF WORRIES

There is a song called "When I Think of His Goodness," and it talks about how God has done so much for us that it makes us want to praise Him. It's so true; when I think about His goodness, I can't help but get happy. That is a great truth for whenever you feel frustrated, a little upset, a bit worried or anxious, or maybe when you don't even understand what you're feeling—you just know it's not good. God understands that. He completely understands you—and He loves you. Ask Him to help, and He will. He delights in putting joy in your heart when you need it.

One of my prayers is that believers everywhere would know the absolute joy and delight of God—of His joy and delight in them, and of their joy and delight in Him. There's a joy that causes your face to shine and your eyes to sparkle even when things aren't going well. He wants to so supercharge you that people say, "I want what you have. I want to know God like you know Him." His joy is our strength.

This is true not only in the wilderness but also in the midst of incredible favor. Even when God is doing wonderful things and opening doors all around us, working miracles and restoring lives, it's not enough. Those are certainly wonderful experiences, and I would never downplay them. I thank God for all He is doing, and it's truly amazing. But the cry of our hearts even in those seasons must be, "Oh, Jesus, I want to know You more. I want to be with You, to commune with You, to go deeper with You." That doesn't change. Why? Because knowing Him is not the means to an end, as if once we know Him well enough He will work miracles in our lives and then we don't need to depend on His personal touch anymore. No, our hearts will always cry out, "I get to know Him! How awesome He is! Yes, I get to do wonderful things with Him. But look at Him! He is so much more wonderful than those things."

A New Way of Thinking

I used to analyze things a lot. I would spend a lot of time thinking. One of my thought patterns was to assume God felt the same way about me that other significant people in my life felt about me—the way I had been identified as I grew up. So I would come to Him thinking, "He's probably a bit frustrated with me. He probably thinks I'm sort of an idiot. But I'll come anyway because He loves me. He has to. That's what He does. But I really don't know if He likes me very much."

God takes such delight in changing our perspectives! Bit by bit, He began to speak to me. I had been teaching jazz singing at a music school, and people had started to ask me to sing in their bands and take jobs in the casinos and clubs. I was flattered, and though I didn't take any of the invitations, I continued at the music school. But after a while I knew my heart was getting distracted and the attention was starting to turn my head. I felt that the Lord showed me I needed to leave. But I resisted. I knew I loved Him and would never walk away from Him, so I kept the job because the invitations and the affirmation felt really good. But it was also highlighting the rejection I was experiencing in the church system and feeding the hurt in my heart.

Beware, the enemy will try to subtly turn our hearts away from church and will create opportunities tailored to feed our offenses. There are no perfect churches, but the Word of God is clear about not forsaking the fellowship of the believers. Church can often be the very crucible needed to develop character in our lives. Running away just means going around the mountain again—delaying the time in the furnace needed for promotion.

After about three months of resisting God, I was praying and saw a vision of a bird flying while carrying a string attached to a rock. The Lord spoke clearly: "Katherine, you need to cut that off. It's not doing you any good. If you are going to go higher, you will have to let this go. I want you to give it up."

This word was a shock because it was so clear. I went in immediately and resigned from the job. But I beat myself up for weeks afterward. Why had it taken me so long to quit? I had felt the nudge much earlier and had done nothing about it. I was supposed to be called to ministry, and I couldn't even be obedient to a simple instruction I had been sensing for three months. It took me that long to listen to Him!

I recall going to a worship service during this time and seeing the people around me laughing hysterically and shaking and falling. My heart was burning; I had come because I wanted more of Him. I felt like crying. But all these people around me seemed to be having an incredibly good time. The more they laughed, the more I would cry. I had been feeling sorry for myself, thinking there was something wrong with me, that I just didn't get it, that I couldn't understand God at all. So I was very serious about seeking Him. These laughing people weren't serious at all. I got very annoyed with them because they didn't seem to be seeking the face of God as I was. But my heart still burned, and I told God that if that's what He wanted, I would do it. I would try to laugh like everyone else.

God wasn't interested in making me do something. He didn't want me to manufacture a response to Him. He wanted me to change my thinking. I was beating myself up for being so slow to respond to Him. I still had the mentality that I would have to do something to make Him happy with me. I wasn't living up to His standards very well, so how could He not be frustrated with me? I thought I would put myself in the naughty corner for a few weeks, trying to punish myself. If only I could repent properly, I could perhaps earn the privilege of being able to experience Him. I figured my sin must have been what kept me from encountering Him like everyone else did. If I could overcome that, then maybe I could laugh.

One night I went forward, crying while everyone

around me was laughing and enjoying themselves, and I begged Him, "Please, Jesus, help me. I feel so condemned. I have let You down so many times."

Later at home, still saying these things to the Lord, I went to the piano and began to write a song. Actually, God was writing the song to me: "You think you've fallen too far from grace. You hear my voice, and you still hide your face in shame. But I've covered your sin; I've taken your shame; I've paid all your debts; now I'm calling your name."[3] I began to believe Him and thanked Him.

The next time I went to church, everyone was laughing and I was still crying out, "Oh, I'm so hungry!" The Lord came and touched me, and I was slain in the Spirit. And as I lay on the floor crying, I turned my head and opened my eyes, and I saw an open vision of Jesus's face. He wasn't looking at me harshly at all. He was looking at me with eyes that were so full of love—those soft eyes that people who are head-over-heels in love have for each other. I will never forget His eyes so full of kindness—I was overwhelmed and undone by His love. I found myself laughing and laughing as my burdens lifted and the condemnation washed away. No one could hear me because I had laryngitis at the time, which was weird but wonderful. I could finally laugh as others were laughing.

It can take time for thought patterns to change, so God continued to convince me that He was not out to get me. He wasn't ganging up on me, He wasn't waiting for me to fail so He could point out how badly I missed it again, and He wasn't thinking up punishments for me to experience if I didn't punish myself strongly enough. No, He was waiting for me to get over it so He could love me.

I've learned from hard experience that one of the enemy's deadliest traps is to draw you into a religious mindset that says you aren't doing well enough. No matter how hard you try, you will always fall short. I fell victim to this thinking many times through the years. In my early twenties, if someone complimented me on my hair, I'd go home and worry about becoming vain. I'd practically convince myself I should cut my hair off and that God probably wanted me to do that in order to remain humble. And I would never allow myself to feel good about anything for fear of being proud. The more I worried about being proud, the guiltier I felt. I was trapped by my own failing efforts to make myself holy.

That's ridiculous, isn't it? And it's a no-win situation. No matter what you do, there's always a downside to consider. The standards are impossibly high, so you're always falling short. If you fast, it's not long enough. If you give, it's not generously enough. If you witness, you used the wrong words or didn't share with enough people. You get caught in a never-ending effort to do the impossible.

> *One of the enemy's deadliest traps is to draw you into a religious mind-set that says you aren't doing well enough.*

If you buy into a mentality like that, you'll quench all the life out of yourself. There is no freedom there. You'll refuse to dream or even to desire. You'll end up in a wilderness that doesn't end, and there is no grace in that desert. That's why these are such deadly lies from the enemy. He wants you to believe you can somehow earn the favor of God, and then every step of the way he'll convince you that you didn't.

Is it possible to grow in grace and favor? Of course it is; Jesus did. But it wasn't by earning the Father's pleasure. It was by knowing the Father and prioritizing relationship with Him. As you come to know the Father and begin to recognize how He looks at you, you will no longer see eyes of anger or frustration. You will see an invitation to let go and enjoy His presence. You'll begin to understand that He is always happy to see you.

It's in that place of absolute joy that we begin to believe—truly, deeply believe—in the goodness and mercy of God. And when we believe that, we begin to exercise the kind of faith that pleases God. Jesus said the work He wants us to do is to believe on the Son (John 6:29). In fact, Jesus came specifically because we could never measure up. He measured up on our behalf. The law teaches us that we cannot achieve complete holiness on our own. So when we repent of our sins and put our faith in Jesus Christ as our Savior, we become identified with His death, burial, and resurrection, and we get raised into His life, becoming new and taking on His righteousness by faith. You please God when you humble yourself and say, "Thank You, Lord, I know that without You I am weak, but in You I am strong. I believe in You and Your goodness. Help me recognize and know Your love."

I speak often on the apostolic prayer of Ephesians 3:14–21, and this is why. It shows that Paul's great prayer for all the saints was that they would know every dimension of God's love. I prayed it for three months solid because I knew I needed to know this. I battled insecurity and feelings of rejection, and I knew only perfect love could cast out my fears. So I prayed the following passage diligently, believing I was receiving as I prayed.

> For this reason I bow my knees before the Father, from whom every family in heaven and on earth derives its name, that He would grant you, according to the riches of His glory, to be strengthened with power through His Spirit in the inner man, so that Christ may dwell in your hearts through faith; and

that you, being rooted and grounded in love, may
be able to comprehend with all the saints what is
the breadth and length and height and depth, and to
know the love of Christ which surpasses knowledge,
that you may be filled up to all the fullness of God.

Now to Him who is able to do far more abundantly beyond all that we ask or think, according to
the power that works within us, to Him be the glory
in the church and in Christ Jesus to all generations
forever and ever. Amen.
—Ephesians 3:14–21, nas

As I prayed this every day, I personalized it by putting
my name in place of all the pronouns that apply to believers.
The Bible says I can have anything I ask according to the
will of God, and this is clearly God's will. So I knew He
would give this to me. Even when I was going to those
worship meetings that frustrated me, I would begin to let
go and let God love me, believing that He actually wanted
to love me. He let me see the look in His eyes when He
gazed at me, and that was very much an answer to this
prayer. He let me know He was happy that I came. And I
know now that every time I approach Him, He is happy to
see me. Every time I pray, I know He rejoices at the sound
of my voice even more than I delight in hearing His.

I strongly encourage you to pray this prayer and to
believe that this is how God sees you. He is not looking to
condemn you for hypocrisy; He wants to convince you of
your new identity. He wants you to know that as a result
of your faith in His saving grace—that magnificent divine
exchange—you have become the righteousness of God in
Christ, and He's delighted that you have stepped toward
Him. There is no frustration in His gaze. It's pure delight.
And He is so pleased that you've come.

As you believe this, God's perfect love will begin to cast

out all fear. I remember worshipping Him one night and having an amazing time in His presence. I woke up the next day singing songs in my heart to Him. (He loves to give us songs and speak through them. I tell people that if they find a random song going through their heads, sing a little bit and follow the words, because God may be trying to say something through them.) But on this morning it was more than a message of words. As I began singing some of the songs to Him that were bubbling up in my heart, I suddenly felt His presence so strongly that it pinned me to the bed. I could hardly move or even breathe. I couldn't speak or sing anymore. And then He began to sing through me.

This is the song that came out of me: "I kiss You with clean lips, O Lord, lips that You've given to me. I kiss You with clean lips, O Lord, because Your grace is sufficient for me." And then I couldn't speak, sing, or move again. The weighty glory of God was all over me. It was as if He said, "Think about what I just said through you. You can kiss Me with clean lips because My grace is sufficient for you."

This is God's heart for you. He wants you to know that your faith in Jesus, the Savior and Redeemer, is enough. What Jesus did in living and dying for you is sufficient. When He said, "It is finished," He meant that His grace was enough to cover any sin you bring to Him. If we confess our sins, He is faithful and just to forgive us our sins and cleanse us from all unrighteousness (1 John 1:9). Now when you look at Him, He is looking back with pure delight in His eyes, and He thinks you are altogether lovely.

Think about that when you are going through the wilderness, whatever it happens to look like at any given point in your life. Can the fulfillment of your dreams really satisfy you the way He does? He wants to fill you, flood you, and overwhelm you with joy—even before the dreams are accomplished. He wants face-to-face time with you to breathe new life into you and restore your soul. You can have times of refreshing even in the middle of a desert or the Valley of Tears. The enemy may have intended the valley as a means to steal, kill, and destroy. That's his modus operandi; he's out to discourage you. But the Lord will look at you in that exact same place and fill you with strength and joy.

> *Your identity is not in what you have or haven't done. It's in Him and what He has done.*

Brother Yun, the exiled leader of house churches in China, wrote about times in prison when Christians were not allowed to talk with each other. They experienced very distressing times of wilderness, and they couldn't even speak words of encouragement. So whenever they had the opportunity, they would look at each other and draw strength from each other's eyes. The gaze itself would renew them, even when all other circumstances were discouraging.[4]

That is a beautiful illustration of what God does for us. Are you wandering somewhere between the promise and the fulfillment? Are you wondering where God is in your hardships? Do you feel the weight of falling short or missing the mark? Look to God and draw strength from His eyes. His gaze can communicate far more than words ever could. It will burn into you the absolute conviction that He is for you. He doesn't wink at sin, but that isn't His focus. He looks at you to remind you of who you actually are. Your identity is not in what you have or haven't done. It's in Him and what He has done.

Remember, it's no longer you who live but Christ who

lives in you. So in gazing at Him, you are gazing at your life, the source of all your strength and hope. He cannot deny Himself, and that includes His own life in you. You are now His body. He cannot possibly be against you because He is in you, and He can't deny Himself. He wants to refresh you, encourage you, stand with you, and convince you of your righteousness in Him. Then you can begin to walk, look, and smell like Him. You become the aroma of Christ to those who are perishing, rather than being obsessed with the smell of your own weaknesses and failures. You are fully aware and fully awake in Him.

Lies in the Wilderness

None of these glorious truths deny the fact that we actually go through wildernesses. People get nervous when talking about blessing and favor, as though we aren't preparing each other well enough for suffering. Believe me, I have some understanding of suffering, but it was hope in His goodness that helped me get through the hard places. In those times, we must be careful not to lean on our own understanding in trying to explain why we or anyone else is going through a hardship. God said He was well pleased with Jesus right before He led him into the desert to be tempted. Job was not being punished when he went through suffering. For all the trials the disciples endured, it was not because they needed to be corrected. Yet in our ignorance and arrogance, sometimes we can assume we know the purpose of pain in our lives or in the lives of others. Suffering does not mean that God is not pleased with us, just as blessings don't necessarily mean He approves of everything we are doing.

In times of intense pain and trial, I have found people who I thought would sympathize with me behaving more like Job's misguided friends, suggesting in the midst of my agony that I must have done something wrong to have such horrible things happen to me or my family. When I went through a really difficult situation with one of my children, I had people who hardly knew anything about our family suggest that I must have sacrificed my children on the altar of ministry. Adding insult to injury, these people magnified my pain. As it was, I was spending night after night until the wee hours of the morning agonizing with God and desperately trying to think of what I could have or should have done or not done to prevent the circumstances I was facing. The enemy was using these false assumptions to fuel the fire of condemnation.

We can all be judgmental. The disciples fell into this trap. When they saw a man born blind, they automatically assumed his blindness was the result of someone's sin. They asked Jesus who was at fault—the man's father, mother, or the man himself. It was a ridiculous question considering that the man had been born blind! But Jesus stopped all their whys by responding that it was for none of those reasons, and He proceeded to tell them that He was going to heal the man. It is not up to us to try to work out the *why*. Our job is to look to *what* God is going to do. God is more interested in helping us focus on Him as the answer than on the tormenting question of why the difficult circumstance arose in the first place. And trying to judge the why in others' circumstances is rarely helpful, when Jesus just wants to be their answer. We can learn from our mistakes, but in the midst of pain, our best focus is not on the why, but on who Christ is to us in the midst of it all.

During this time of pain and sadness, my first reaction was to give up ministry altogether. But as I agonized in prayer, God spoke to me from the Book of Matthew. I read the story of how Jesus responded when He heard of His cousin John's death. He went to a deserted place by

Himself, probably to grieve. But the crowds followed Him, and Jesus had compassion on them. He healed them, taught them, and fed all five thousand of them. God spoke to me not to withdraw but to have compassion on the people and continue ministering. I praise God now that I did, because the trial lasted five years. I could have spent five years in depression, doing nothing but mourning. Instead, those five years became part of the most fruitful season I had ever had. Then God began to gloriously redeem the time and circumstances to make the situation better than it had ever been. God gives double for our trouble when we choose to keep our eyes on Him rather than on the pain we are feeling. And the comfort we receive from the Holy Spirit in those times is comfort we can then share with others. God does make miracles out of messes for those who will trust Him.

> *Our best focus is not on the why, but on who Christ is to us in the midst of it all.*

In this world we do have troubles. But Jesus tells us to take heart and be encouraged because He has overcome the world (John 16:33). He makes all things work together for the good of those who love Him and are called according to His purpose (Rom. 8:28). That means we can be happy—*even in the middle of a wilderness.*

Don't let the enemy convince you that you're disqualified from experiencing the promises in any of these verses. I used to read Romans 8:28 and think, "Well, do I love Him enough to qualify for this promise?" That was the enemy, of course, once again trying to put an impossible standard on me and telling me I didn't measure up. But nothing we bring to God, including our love, comes from us in the first place. We love because He first loved us

(1 John 4:19). In fact, even if our heart condemns us, He is greater than our heart (1 John 3:20).

There have been a lot of lies told about Jesus, and when you're in a wilderness, it's tempting to believe them. Human beings tend to judge God by our circumstances rather than judging our circumstances by Him, and our circumstances can be a very unreliable measure of who He is. The religious-sounding words about why you're in the wilderness or how God wants you to remain there and endure it paint an unfair picture. God is *for* you. If you want to talk about unfairness, know that it's unfair how very much He loves and adores you. By human standards, this isn't justice. But because of what Jesus did, God gets to do for you what He has always longed to do—to give you the kingdom as a co-heir with Christ and love you with such a strong love that you need supernatural strength to handle it. Regardless of any other voices you've heard, this is the truth about Him.

Spend some time thinking about who God is and who He is for you. It's always good to do that, but it's especially important when you're going through a dry and barren place. That is when distortions about Him are easiest to swallow. Choose to believe the truth. When you wake up, remind yourself that His mercy is new every morning. Know that He isn't looking to see how well you do; He's waiting to see whether you'll have faith in His goodness so He can come in, overwhelm you, and fill you with joy and strength, allowing you to arise and shine as one of His glorious ones. Instead of buying the lies that you're supposed to walk around weak and frail, yield your weakness to Him and let Him clothe you with power from on high. If God is for you, who can be against you?

You are meant to thrive in the wilderness, not just survive in it. And receiving God's love—looking into His eyes and seeing how He really feels about you—gives you power to thrive in even the driest places. Until you get a revelation of His love that fills you to overflowing with His fullness, just as Paul's prayer in Ephesians 3 says, you won't experience His joy. You won't be able to live in the confidence that He wants to do ridiculously good things for you. Until you allow Him to lavish love on you, you won't be able to enter into the fullness of His desire to do exceedingly abundantly beyond all you can ask or think (Eph. 3:20).

This is why so many believers are wandering in the wilderness without experiencing hope or joy. Sadly, for some people the wilderness has become a place of distortion, full of lies about God, when in fact it is where faith gets tested and grows strong. But it can only grow strong when we know God's love, because love is the root of faith. We can only trust someone we love, and we can only love God in response to His love for us. So getting His love is not just a nice thing to encourage us. It isn't just a celebration without any fruit. It's vital. It enables us to receive God's promises by faith, and those promises become our food in barren places.

That's what I was missing in those meetings where everyone was laughing and I was so serious about seeking God. I missed the point. The point is that when you really get the love of God, you actually open doors for faith to be released to see the kingdom of God established on earth.

The busier I become, the more I recognize that I need to schedule time to be loved—to simply look into God's eyes and receive His goodness. You can never be too busy to receive. The busier you are, the more of Him you need. His pleasure over you is like a river, and it never stops flowing.

If you've ever wondered how someone can be satisfied and fulfilled while still in the wilderness, this is the secret. The dreams God has given you will be satisfying and fulfilling, but not nearly as much as He is. Those dreams may take a while to unfold; mine took years, as did the dreams and callings of Joseph, Moses, David, and many more. But God is available now. His love is for every moment, no matter how barren the landscape is. And only He can truly satisfy.

Chapter 4

OVERCOMING
TEMPTATION

I RECENTLY WENT TO lunch with my middle daughter, Emily, and we read poetry. That may seem like an odd lunch activity to some people, but we both really enjoy the beauty of words and how poetry can paint a picture with them, so we had a lovely time reading and eating lunch. One verse stood out to us in one of the poems we read, and it led to a good discussion. The verse says,

> Sound, sound the clarion, fill the fife!
> Throughout the sensual world proclaim,
> One crowded hour of glorious life
> Is worth an age without a name.

That sounds very artistic and profound, doesn't it? It is, but not necessarily in the way it first appears. This poem from the 1700s—"The Call" by Thomas Osbert Mordaunt—is a bit tongue-in-cheek, a sarcastic jab at those who are running off to war and trying to fit as much life in as they can by going out to get drunk and mess around with people. They were trying to convince themselves that one crowded hour of life was worth an age without a name, and the author was beginning to question this hollow lie of hedonism.

Hedonism is the philosophy that the pursuit of pleasure is the highest value, and humanistic hedonism usually defines pleasure in terms of sensual self-indulgence.

It says sensuality is the ultimate good and the proper aim of human life. It's the "if it feels good, do it" philosophy. Just please yourself. And many, many people are living this lie today.

The reality is that what people think they want is usually not what they really want. Very often what people seek to satisfy their desires is actually a substitute for what they're really craving. As God is leading us in the process through the wilderness toward the wonders He has placed before us, our temporal desires can become really distorted. We are tempted to pursue things we think we want, when what we really want is available in Christ. Our surface desires distract us. Remember, only He can satisfy. Yet it's so easy to look for other things to satisfy us when we are in the wilderness.

Humanistic hedonism is an extreme form of this, as people try to fill their deep craving for love and meaning with pleasures, possessions, and other people. But there are so many much more subtle ways to reach for desires that won't ultimately fulfill us. Sometimes the dreams God has given us can take the place of God in our lives. Sometimes, when both our deep and our surface desires are not being fulfilled, we are tempted to give in to discouragement and frustration, and we lose heart. The wilderness can be a dangerous place for our faith, and the opportunities to choose something other than our true calling seem to grow larger and larger. We will never walk in the wonders God has called us to walk in if we give in to the wilderness temptations. We have to persevere in the hope set before us.

Create the Path

God wants your breakthroughs to happen. He wouldn't have imparted dreams and desires to you if He didn't want to fulfill them. But He's after something even more significant than the fulfillment of those things. He wants to release genuine joy in your life before breakthrough happens.

Many people are trying to live the life of faith while walking in anxiety. God wants us to begin to sing songs in the desert. If you're looking for a breakthrough, start imagining what it's going to look like when it happens, and begin to worship Him. Rejoice over what He is doing, even when it doesn't seem like anything is happening. One of the greatest things you can do in the desert is to sing about what you haven't seen yet.

That isn't just an empty exercise. Looking at what you haven't seen come to pass yet will help you begin to focus on hope. You allow your emotions to go there as though it was already happening. Rejoicing isn't something you pretend to do; you actually begin to sense the reality of what is coming. God wants to release joy about your future to you long before it happens. He wants to bring you into the place where you get so genuinely happy about what you know He is going to do that it's as if He has already done it.

In that place of joy, you actually begin to create. You work with God as a co-laborer to create the path on which He will deliver the promise. It's the Holy Spirit's faith that pleases God, and this is what His faith looks like. It's true hope.

> *One of the greatest things you can do in the desert is to sing about what you haven't seen yet.*

In English we use the word *hope* for many different things. We hope for nice weather, a certain Christmas present, a wish fulfilled. "I hope so" can apply to almost anything we look forward to, whether it's minor or major, realistic or delusional, a faint wish or a solid expectation, or anything in between.

In the Bible hope is more certain than it is in English. When the Bible speaks of hope, it isn't talking about a wish. A wish does not contain the assurance of fulfillment, and often when we think we are hoping we are actually wishing that God would do something. In Scripture hope is genuinely joyful about a future certainty that you have haven't yet seen (Heb. 11:1). Whether it will come to pass isn't in question. Hope is the anticipation of God's goodness as it will be expressed in the future, and leaves no room for anxious thinking.

This is not the kind of hope you have to spend a lot of energy whipping up in yourself, as if you're trying to convince yourself of something that isn't likely to happen. This isn't a wish that is backed by fear and worry. Hope is genuine joy, the assurance that something will come to pass because God is faithful. *That's* where God wants our hearts to live all the time, no matter what desert we're passing through.

So hope is not vague, it's not for the fainthearted, and it's not only for seasons of abundance. In fact, we get an entirely different view from Scripture:

> Therefore, having been justified by faith, we have peace with God through our Lord Jesus Christ, through whom also we have access by faith into this grace in which we stand, and rejoice in hope of the glory of God. And not only that, but we also glory in tribulations, knowing that tribulation produces perseverance; and perseverance, character; and character, hope. Now hope does not disappoint, because the love of God has been poured out in our hearts by the Holy Spirit who was given to us.
>
> —ROMANS 5:1–5, NKJV

Do you see the context for this hope? It comes in the fiery trials of life, in the barren deserts and valleys of tears, in the middle of the process rather than only at the end. And the beautiful ending of this passage reminds us not only that hope grows out of our experience of God's love but also that it does not disappoint. It's a rock-solid certainty.

The Message translates hope as "alert expectancy." I love that. As you set your face like flint in order to persevere; as you choose to go through the barren deserts rather than trying to get around them; as you deliberately ignore the temptations of pleasure, distraction, or disappointment, God strengthens you, fills you with expectancy, and produces in you the kind of hope that does not disappoint.

The prophet Habakkuk has a beautiful way of saying this. God gives you hind's feet for high places (Hab. 3:19). In other words, He gives you the ability to ascend rocky, treacherous places with grace and sure feet. Where most people would fall, you stand. Where many would choose not to climb, you are able to dance. You are called to the heights, the high places of influence, and hope takes you there.

Don't Lose Heart

Habakkuk knew a thing or two about temptation in the wilderness. The temptations he faced were not of the hedonistic variety, with pleasures and sensuality calling out to him with false sources of strength. No, his temptations were discouragement and a sense of futility. He looked at the evil around him and asked God why He didn't do something about it. But he didn't lose heart. At the end of his prophecy he gives us a wonderful expression of what it means to resist temptation in the wilderness and cling to certain hope:

> Though the fig tree does not bud and there are no
> grapes on the vines, though the olive crop fails
> and the fields produce no food, though there are
> no sheep in the pen and no cattle in the stalls, yet
> I will rejoice in the LORD, I will be joyful in God
> my Savior. The Sovereign LORD is my strength; he
> makes my feet like the feet of a deer, he enables me
> to tread on the heights.
>
> —HABAKKUK 3:17–19

These words came from the prophet's pen before victory blossomed, before there was any fruit on the vine, before he saw any of God's promises come to pass. That's where God gives hind's feet for high places. It's worth whatever you're going through, because on the other side it's going to be glorious. Perseverance produces character, character produces hope—alert expectancy—and hope does not disappoint. Why? Because God has poured His love into our hearts by His Spirit, and His perfect love casts out fear.

This is how we overcome wilderness temptations. The Bible gives us plenty of examples of people who did—Abraham, Joseph, Moses, David, and many others—as well as some examples of those who didn't. One who didn't was Esau, the brother of Jacob, whose story is told in Genesis:

> Once when Jacob was cooking some stew, Esau
> came in from the open country, famished. He said
> to Jacob, "Quick, let me have some of that red stew!
> I'm famished!" (That is why he was also called
> Edom.)
>
> Jacob replied, "First sell me your birthright."
>
> "Look, I am about to die," Esau said. "What good
> is the birthright to me?"
>
> But Jacob said, "Swear to me first." So he swore
> an oath to him, selling his birthright to Jacob. Then
> Jacob gave Esau some bread and some lentil stew.

> He ate and drank, and then got up and left. So Esau
> despised his birthright.
>
> —GENESIS 25:29–34

Esau wasn't really about to die—not simply for a lack of stew. He was exaggerating, just like a teenager who heads straight for the refrigerator when he gets home from school. He was hungry, and his appetite took first priority. Like hedonists who seek pleasure in a misguided attempt to cover their pain or fulfill their deepest longings, Esau was willing to give up his birthright in order to satisfy his appetite. He gave in to temptation—apparently without much of a fight.

That's what often happens when what we think we want isn't actually what we want. For the moment, Esau didn't care about anything else. His flesh was crying out, he could smell the aroma of temptation, and his eyes were fixed on his empty stomach and a pot of stew. He took his gaze off his future and looked exclusively at his present wants. That's all it took.

If Esau had really thought that satisfying a temporary, momentary desire was going to cost him his birthright, he wouldn't have bargained away his future. But the wilderness tends to distort our values that way, doesn't it? It tempts us to live for the moment. "Just do it. Live for the moment. Satisfying your immediate desires will be good." But it isn't good at all because it undermines our future and robs us of blessing. Later on, Esau deeply regretted what he did and sought his blessing with tears (Heb. 12:17), but it was too late. He missed a lifelong opportunity because of a temporary hunger.

Do you see why the enemy fills our wilderness seasons with temptations to satisfy fleeting desires or to give up on our hope? There's a lot at stake. He has an inkling of the dreams and desires God has imparted to you, and he doesn't want them to be fulfilled. They—and you—are dangerous to him. He doesn't want you to persevere for the hope set before you. He is afraid of the things that will bring you lasting joy and great delight because those are also the things that will dismantle his kingdom and advance God's.

There is an even more tragic example than Esau of a hedonistic attitude in Scripture. It's the story of two of David's children: Amnon and his half-sister Tamar. Amnon was David's firstborn, and he fell in love with Tamar, a daughter of David and sister of Absalom. He wanted what seemed impossible for him to have, and he became obsessed to the point of sickness.

Amnon got some really bad advice from a cousin on how to get Tamar alone with him. He pretended to be bedridden, and when David came to see him, he requested Tamar as his caretaker to cook for him and feed him. David granted his request.

> So Tamar went to the house of Amnon her brother, where he was lying. She took the dough, kneaded it, and made the cakes before him. Then she baked them. Then she took the baking tray and served the cakes to him, but he refused to eat.
>
> Amnon said, "Send everyone away." So they all left him. Then Amnon said to Tamar, "Bring the food into the bedroom that I may eat from your hand." So Tamar took the cakes that she had made and brought them in the bedroom to Amnon her brother. When she brought them close for him to eat, he took hold of her and said, "Come, lie with me, my sister."
>
> She pled with him, "No, my brother, do not violate me, for such a thing is not to be done in Israel. Do not carry out this awful thing. As for me, where could I escape my disgrace? And you would be like

one of the fools in Israel. Now, please speak to the king, for he will not withhold me from you." But he refused to listen to her. So, being stronger than her, he overpowered her and lay with her.

Then Amnon hated her greatly, so that the hatred with which he hated her was greater than the love with which he had loved her. And Amnon said to her, "Get up, go away."

—2 Samuel 13:8–15, mev

This is a terribly sad story, but it's evidence of what can happen when we start to focus on fleshly desires. Most of us never give in to them as Amnon did, but we experience the same type of dynamic. The enemy comes and tempts. The Bible says God makes a way of escape out of every temptation, but if we start to focus on that sensual desire—that red stew or that unattainable lover—we have a lot of help from unclean spirits who are more than happy to stir up unclean thoughts. God wants to be our help in those situations, but our intense focus on what we want can shut Him out of the process. If instead we can recognize what is going on and resist the thoughts, deliberately casting them out like the intruders they are and putting our gaze back on God, we will find that the Holy Spirit refreshes and strengthens us. He makes a way of escape out of every temptation. He wants to give us counsel and deliver us. He wants to encourage us, to pull us out of the hopelessness that so easily distorts our priorities and fill us with the expectant hope that does not disappoint.

He can do that only if we get real with Him and say, "Lord, I've been feeling tempted in this area. I've gotten discouraged. I've been focused on momentary desires. I've been having these thoughts..." And when we do that, His response is one of delight. "Wonderful! I'm here to help you. Let Me give you strength. Let Me bless you, encourage you, refresh you. I'm not rejecting you because you've been tempted; I'm delighted you asked for My help."

God will often begin to convict us of sin with a still, small voice, and if at that point we will pay attention and yield, repenting and asking Him what to do and how to think instead, we will find the way of escape. In wilderness times, we can become so much more vulnerable to the seemingly comforting voices of people and things that may not be right, and it is vital to take care to listen to our conscience. He wants to be the one we attach to and rely on, and He is jealous when we become dependent on people and things. If you don't listen to His still, small voice, God may have to start speaking to you through friends and leaders to break through the lies you are using to justify yourself. And if you don't listen then, your conscience could be seared, and you may be headed for a public rebuke, which is far more painful.

I have a friend, a well-respected prophet, who was sent to a man of God with a big public ministry. In love, and in private, with only one witness, the prophet told him that the Lord had revealed through a word of knowledge that he was secretly committing serious sin and needed to repent. Instead of repenting, he denied it, and a few months later he was publicly exposed by the secular media and lost his whole ministry. It's a fearful thing when we start to believe our own justifications for sin. We would do well to remember that "your sin will find you out" (Num. 32:23, MEV). God is too good to let you continue down a destructive road without intervention. How you respond is vitally important. God resists the proud but gives grace to the humble. As I said earlier, when it comes to yielding to God, obedience is essential. And it's far better to surrender quickly!

You've seen a couple of examples from Scripture of people who gave in to temptation. Here is one who didn't:

> According to His custom, He came out and went to the Mount of Olives. And His disciples followed Him. When He came there, He said to them, "Pray that you may not fall into temptation." He withdrew from them about a stone's throw, and He knelt down and prayed, "Father, if You are willing, remove this cup from Me. Nevertheless not My will, but Yours, be done." An angel from heaven appeared to Him, strengthening Him. And being in anguish, He prayed more earnestly. And His sweat became like great drops of blood falling down to the ground.
>
> When He rose from prayer and had come to His disciples, He found them sleeping from sorrow. He said to them, "Why do you sleep? Rise and pray, lest you fall into temptation."
>
> —LUKE 22:39–46, MEV

Jesus was being tempted to avoid the Cross, and He was in anguish to the point of tears and blood dripping from His face. Nothing in His flesh wanted to do this. But there was a deeper desire. He wanted to do things God's way because He knew God's way would be worth it. The end result would be glorious. Like Esau and Amnon, He was desperate for something. But He went to the Father and said, "Help Me. Strengthen Me. Not My will but Yours." And in believing God's ways are better than ours, He persevered through the wilderness and endured the Cross.

Hebrews 12 tells us how to follow the same course.

> Therefore, since we are encompassed with such a great cloud of witnesses, let us also lay aside every weight and the sin that so easily entangles us, and let us run with endurance the race that is set before

> us. Let us look to Jesus, the author and finisher of
> our faith, who for the joy that was set before Him
> endured the cross, despising the shame, and is
> seated at the right hand of the throne of God. For
> consider Him who endured such hostility from sin-
> ners against Himself, lest you become weary and
> your hearts give up.
>
> —HEBREWS 12:1–3, MEV

What you actually want—not your fleeting, momentary
desires, however strong they are, but your deepest, truest
longings—are worth waiting for. They are worth whatever
perseverance is required. If you know in your heart that
God has a plan and purpose for your destiny, you know
the future will be glorious. To give in to momentary sensual pleasure or to lose heart in discouragement will rob
you of what God truly has for you. When you fall, He
will be there to help you get back on track, but He would
rather deliver you from that experience before it ever happens. He wants to rescue you from futility and frustration.
And in every situation, He gives a way of escape.

Jesus didn't give up His calling for a pot of stew or a
cheap deliverance from trouble. He wrestled with the
gravity of the situation, but He didn't give in to discouragement. In fact, He went to the Cross "for the joy set
before him" (Heb. 12:2). That's expectant hope. And it sus-
tained Him even in a dark garden on His darkest night.

Christ's experience in the garden is one example of what
Scripture means when it says He was tempted in all the
ways we are. It's also the greatest example of how He over-
came. Because He did, God invites you to come to Him
in complete honesty about all the trials and temptations
you're facing. He can give you His overcoming strength in
your times of trial. He's on your side.

Sadly, many people pull away from God when they start

to go through temptation. Their loneliness in the wilderness causes them to isolate themselves even further—at exactly the times when they need God more than ever. Adam and Eve did that in the garden; they pulled away from God because they felt ashamed. Yet God wants us to run to Him. He is saying, "I went through all that temptation so I could identify with you, so I could overcome in exactly the areas you need to overcome. I wanted you to take My victory for yourself." He wants to give us His strength.

When you're feeling discouraged and depressed, God wants you to come to Him. He knows how vulnerable you are. He knows your weaknesses and tendencies. He wants to give you strength in your difficult situation. He says, "Pray that you don't fall into temptation. Pray that you don't become prey to the enemy in your weakened state. I want to give you strength by being the strength you need."

One of the greatest temptations I faced in the wilderness was the temptation to hate those who were hurting me and those I love. Bitterness and unforgiveness are terrible traps designed to destroy us from the inside out. The devil doesn't play fair. Your sense of justice in the midst of unfair treatment can cause you to want to write speeches in your head and moan to whoever will listen to your terrible plight.

Bless Those Who Curse You

I was in my early thirties and just coming out of a seven-year trial during which I had been tested and misunderstood, falsely accused, and mistreated. And then just as things started to get better, my husband, Tom, became a target. Secondhand offense is so dangerous and can be even worse than offenses you have suffered personally. You can continue to nurse hurts on behalf of the ones you love long after they have forgiven and moved on. My husband, one of the kindest and most noble men I know, was terribly mistreated by people we expected would stand by him and love him.

Expectations are a dangerous thing. When we put expectations on people to behave a certain way, we have no choice but to judge them as to how well they live up to whatever we expected of them. We all do it; we can have expectations of our families, our spouses, our pastors, or our friends. We compare them to others. Our idea of how a mother, father, sister, brother, or spouse should treat us is based on what we learn about other people's families. We convince ourselves that they owe it to us to love us, celebrate us, and support us, and then we judge them when they don't measure up. But the problem with judgment is that we reap what we sow. God has forgiven us and asks us to do the same for others.

I knew the Bible said we should bless those who curse us and pray for those who spitefully use us, and that we must love our enemies. But this seemed like such a difficult concept. I didn't want people who were hurting us to be blessed! There was anger in my heart, and I wanted them to know how awful their behavior was. I figured that if God blessed them, they would never see how wrong they were and would continue to hurt others. I wanted them to be convicted of their sin and to apologize and put things right! The best I felt I could do was pray that God would bless them with conviction of their sin. And as for loving them...well, I certainly didn't feel much love, particularly for those who were hurting my husband. So how do we bless those who curse us? How do we forgive and forget?

Jesus asks us to forgive others' debts even as we have had our own debts forgiven. While we all long to be surrounded by people who value and love us and treat us fairly, there is only one who can live up to our expectations.

God is the perfect Father who loves to give us all the time, attention, affirmation, comfort, help, and support we need. In fact, the Holy Spirit is jealous to fulfill these needs in our lives. As people who have been adopted into God's family, the Father wants us to set our earthly family and friends free from our high standards. Learning how to release people from the expectations of what we feel they owe us is a massive step of growth. By disciplining ourselves to cast down every thought that doesn't line up with the truth of who God is and who we are in Him—those thoughts that are not pure and lovely and of a good report (Phil. 4:8)—we can set our minds on things above and draw on the love that flows from Him.

Stephen, a follower of Jesus, was able to do that as he was being stoned to death; he set his thoughts on his Savior, and love and forgiveness for his enemies overflowed. Instead of being worked up over the sense of injustice (that the Pharisees should have known better), he fixed his eyes on the one from whom love, power, and forgiveness flow. And Jesus, as He was being crucified on the cross and taunted by the ones He came to save, was able to pray for them from a heart overflowing with love and forgiveness. This is a privilege that we have. As children of God, raised up with Christ and given new hearts, we have access to the same love and forgiveness Christ had. From the place of being loved, affirmed, accepted, forgiven, and seated in heavenly places with Him, we can tap into the same love for those who hate us that Jesus has.

> *The Father wants us to set our earthly family and friends free from our high standards.*

We have been forgiven much and have been given the keys of the kingdom and the privilege of being adopted into God's family. Aware of that, forgiving our natural families and releasing them from what we feel they owe us becomes a privilege. We don't want to be like the servant who was forgiven a huge debt only to go out and demand repayment from the one who owed him a small debt. God wants us to be heavenly minded so we are not drawn into the small-mindedness of earthly thinking.

FORGIVENESS IS A CHOICE

The Bible tells us we must forgive one another from the heart. This mandate used to trouble me a great deal, as I would find myself choosing to forgive and then battling thoughts at night about things people had done. Then I would feel bad that I still hadn't forgiven them, so I would try harder to pray and forgive, only to be tempted again with feelings of anger.

Temptation does not define us. Even Jesus was tempted in the wilderness. With our new identity in Christ, we look like He does—righteous, joyful, peaceful, full of love that is patient and kind, and more. We have become the righteousness of God in Christ through faith. Rather than feeling condemned by the fact that we are being tempted, we need to recognize rogue thoughts of unforgiveness as intruders into our thought lives that need to be cast down and replaced with truth.

> *Nothing we learn in the wilderness is wasted; God truly does make all things work together for our good.*

After many sleepless nights battling thoughts of unforgiveness, one night I'd had enough. I got up and wrote out a declaration on a piece of paper. I declared that by the grace of God I forgave (I named the people), and that

I released them from the debts of the apologies I felt they owed. I declared that I was moving on into the future He had for me and letting go of past pain. I declared that I loved them and blessed them. Then when the enemy would try to come and replay the video of past hurts in my mind as I tried to go to sleep, I would get up, show him the piece of paper in my drawer, and tell him I was not going back there again!

We have the opportunity in the wilderness to learn lessons and gain experiences we will need to handle the high winds that often blow on the high places God wants to promote us to. When I first started driving, my mother arranged for me to take a defensive driving course. The instructors would take you out to an oily patch of road and deliberately cause your car to slide in order to teach you how to get out of a situation when your wheels lost traction. We did it several times, and then years later, when I found myself on a slippery road, I was surprised how automatic my reaction was. I had experienced the feeling of slipping before and knew what to do. In the same way, when we learn how to forgive and guard our hearts in the early years, in the later times—when the stakes are higher, our influence is greater, and the tests are harder—we have a default setting to forgive and love that we learned on the oil skids of life. Nothing we learn in the wilderness is wasted; God truly does make all things work together for our good.

Overcoming the Opposition

The wisdom we gain as we journey with God is invaluable, and I thank God for each lesson I have learned with Him along the way. Sometimes when I travel somewhere to minister, I experience demonic activity when I arrive in the region. Occasionally I'll even get an attack or an intimidating dream in the middle of the night and wonder what is going on. But I've discovered through experience with God that this is fairly normal. Often when I am about to see breakthrough in a region, spiritual opposition is sent to intimidate or distract me. And rather than just battle with it all night long, I'm starting to recognize it up front and deal with it. I've also learned the value of having intercessors! I know God has already brought victory, I resist the attack, and I rebuke the demonic spirit that is trying to intimidate me. I see it as an intruder in my room and tell it to get out in the name of Jesus. Then I release the peace of God into the room. I'll drift off to sleep again reminding myself of who God is and what I look like in Him.

Scripture says that when you enter a house, you are to let your peace come upon it. You have the authority as an ambassador of Christ to release peace—literally *shalom*, the fullness, wholeness, and abundance of God—wherever you go. This is really an act of spiritual warfare, but very often without the drama most people associate with that. You can calmly take authority in whatever space you're in right now and release the peace of God into it. Rather than talking up the enemy as if he's impressive—you know how some people enjoy describing how ominous their spiritual warfare is—you actually do something about it. Instead of giving the enemy credit for his power, you simply say, "I release peace in the name of Jesus. I command every spirit that is not of God to go."

Begin to recognize when opposition comes. It often manifests in the form of overwhelming discouragement, bad dreams, or temptation, but it's actually an evil spirit sent to try to hinder you on your God-given assignment. Say no to it and tell the devil you are not going there. Choose to run the race and receive the prize. Choose the joy set before you. Ask the Holy Spirit for the strength to do all that God has called you to do, and receive the strength He gives.

When you make those choices day by day, hour by hour, even moment by moment, pulling on God for supernatural strength, you not only get the joy of seeing the dreams and desires He has given you come to pass; He also delights in adding all the blessings He wants into your life because He recognizes that you will no longer attach to unworthy things. You've chosen the better thing. You have said with David, "One thing I have desired of the LORD, that will I seek: That I may dwell in the house of the LORD all the days of my life, to behold the beauty of the LORD, and to inquire in His temple" (Ps. 27:4, NKJV). You've staked your hope on the truth that only God can satisfy.

BREAKTHROUGH IS COMING

I really believe the Spirit is about to bring breakthrough to many who have been wandering in a wilderness and are learning to resist temptation, not lose heart, and keep their focus on Him. I believe God wants you right now to recognize that there are all sorts of things trying to divert your attention. Your birthright is under attack. But as you fix your eyes on Jesus, the author and finisher of your faith, the one who is your hope and who has extraordinary plans for you, you will endure. You'll even thrive. Breakthrough will come.

It is very easy when you have experienced disappointment—when the things you've been hoping for don't come to pass—to give in to the temptation to be depressed or bitter, or to comfort yourself with pleasures that will not satisfy you in the long run. But the reality is that those pleasures cannot fill your deep longings. They cannot take away any disappointments you have felt or distract you from your true calling in any satisfying way. They are temporary—just as your wilderness is temporary. And you never really want to make lifelong sacrifices to address a temporary need or desire.

Whenever the enemy tries to discourage me about things that have not yet come to pass, I take the approach Peter took in John 6:68. Where else am I going to go? Jesus alone has the words of life. I remind myself that it doesn't matter what circumstances look like right now. Really, where else would I go? Would I run off with the enemy to have a pity party? Buy into the lie of "eat, drink, and be merry, for tomorrow we die"? The reality is that these temptations lead to death. Humanistic hedonism is a lie. Self-pity accomplishes nothing. It's all empty except for Jesus. He has the words of eternal life. He gives hope. He overcomes.

God is looking for us to make the choice Jesus made: "Not my will, Lord, but Yours be done, because Your ways lead to abundant life. I choose life and receive Your supernatural strength. I place my hope in the joy set before me." God is so faithful to meet you there in that choice. He delights to do so. He wants to encourage you as you feed on His faithfulness.

If you're in that place where His promises have not yet come to pass, begin to focus on His goodness. Take your eyes off any other distractions or temptations and start to give thanks for what you have seen Him do. Remind yourself of the ways in which He has been good to you. Think about what He has promised to do. Let it become real in the eyes of your heart. Let your imagining of what will be—that expectant hope of what is certain—grow larger than your vision of the actual circumstances you're moving through right now. As you do, you can enter into the genuine joy of what you see coming.

There is no way around the fact that inheriting the promises of God requires faith and patience (Heb. 6:12). So don't be alarmed simply because the process involves faith and patience. Wilderness experiences are normal. God gives the opportunity, He has offered an invitation of a prophetic destiny, and it's up to you to choose to say yes to Him. But saying yes involves persevering, hoping with certainty, and rejecting whatever comes into conflict with your inheritance. This choice is so very worth it. What God has for you is better than you have ever, ever imagined.

Chapter 5

MAINTAINING INTEGRITY IN THE FACE OF INJUSTICE

OSEPH SHARED HIS dreams with his family, and his brothers betrayed him by selling him to slave-traders. He spent the next years as a slave and then as a prisoner, the dreams God had given him seemingly out of reach. He had plenty of time to be offended, focus on the betrayal, and nurse bitterness. Years later, God even gave him opportunity to retaliate. But Joseph showed no signs of bitterness, and instead of retaliating he blessed his family.

David had been anointed by God's priest as the next king. But instead of waiting in the royal courts to assume the throne, he was forced into the wilderness. Saul, his king and father-in-law, pursued him relentlessly to kill him. It was a horribly unjust situation. Like Joseph, David had plenty of opportunities to become bitter, and he even had two chances to retaliate. But also like Joseph, he didn't. He trusted God and waited for His timing.

Jesus, the sinless Son of God, experienced the worst injustice in history—being executed by sinful human beings. Yet even while He was being nailed to the cross, He asked the Father to forgive His tormentors because "they [did] not know what they [were] doing" (Luke 23:34). He later looked at Peter, who had fiercely denied Him, and forgave and restored him—without any bitterness. (See John 21:15–19.)

In fact, the Bible is full of people who suffered injustice, and how they responded to it demonstrated something about their relationship with God. How they responded to these injustices determined the blessings they walked into. Almost everyone God used greatly for His kingdom experienced some type of injustice or offense.

Sometimes our wilderness seasons include an experience of injustice, and how we respond in those moments may affect how long the wilderness lasts. Will we focus on the unfairness, the false accusation, the loss, or the offense? Or will we lift our gaze and keep our eyes on the prize? Joseph could have been tormented by his brothers' treachery, and David could have been tormented by Saul's injustices. But both maintained their own integrity even when they had opportunities to retaliate. Jesus could have condemned those who persecuted Him, but He endured the Cross for the joy set before Him. God responds to such integrity with His presence and power.

POWER IN FORGIVENESS

Christians are good about knowing that Jesus came into the world to forgive us of our sins. It is a wonderful truth that He purchased salvation for us. But many people forget the reality that not only did He come to forgive us of sins; He also came to make us new creatures. He gives us His heart and His nature. His Spirit comes to live inside of us, and we then have the power to love as He loves and forgive as He forgives. We actually have the power to be as He is in this world (1 John 4:17).

There is tremendous power in that truth. Being as He is in this world is a comprehensive opportunity. We don't just select the miraculous part of His work; we embrace His loving and forgiving nature too. And there's a strong connection between those who walk in love and forgiveness and those who walk in miracles. Like those in Scripture who experienced injustice in the wilderness without becoming bitter, learning how to forgive people in our wilderness prepares us to live in power when we come out of it.

Most of us don't experience betrayals as offensive as those Joseph, David, and Jesus experienced. Our encounters with injustice come more often in day-to-day life with family, friends, and coworkers. And we forget the reality that we've been given the power to forgive others of their debts.

Every one of us has been forgiven of an enormous debt. Isn't that wonderful? In Jesus, everything I've ever done wrong was forgiven when I repented and received His grace, and if you are a follower of Christ, so has everything you've ever done. But then God says to forgive our debtors in the same way we've been forgiven of our debts. Instead, we often put expectations on others, particularly those closest to us. We come up with expectations of what a mother or father should be like, what a son or daughter should be like, or what a friend or pastor or business associate should be like. These expectations give us a sense that the people in our lives owe us something. We would never say that because our assumptions work so subtly within us. But we put people in a box of "shoulds"—"He should do this," or, "She shouldn't be like that." Then, when those people don't measure up to our expectations, we judge them for falling short.

Every "should" eventually leads to a judgment. The person either measures up to our expectations or doesn't. Our hearts fill up with unconscious debts. But the Holy Spirit wants us to forgive everyone of those debts, and we need to be really careful to do so. He has freed us from that system of judgment by forgiving all our debts. It isn't right to accept freedom from that system and then apply it to others. We are living as princes and princesses of the Most High God who have the privilege of loving and forgiving as He loves and forgives. It's up to us to release debts.

I believe God wants us to be able to cancel others' debts in the same way our own debts have been cancelled. That is what Jesus's parable of the unmerciful servant teaches us (Matt. 18:21–35). The servant who was forgiven an enormous debt went out and mercilessly collected minor debts from others, and his master eventually held him accountable. We need to be people who wake up and recognize that debt cancellation is our business. It sets people free and allows God to love them through us.

People instinctively know when we hold judgments against them, even when we don't verbalize them. Anything in our hearts eventually comes out in some form. Our "shoulds" and expectations keep us from loving people the way God loves them, and if we are hindered from walking in His love, we are hindered from walking in His power. The two go hand-in-hand.

> *I believe God wants us to be able to cancel others' debts in the same way our own debts have been cancelled.*

I am not suggesting that we wink at sin and refuse to acknowledge things that are wrong. Discernment is a gift from God that enables us to say, "This should not be." But we have to be very careful not to judge people in our discernment of right and wrong. We can recognize the evil people might do without holding their sins against them. Even when people have committed genuine offenses against us—as Joseph's brothers did to him and Saul did to David—we choose to release them from our judgment and give up our expectations of who they ought to be. We have to make the most of our opportunities to love.

Our drive to develop expectations for other people comes from our own need for identity and value. Our expectations come from our woundedness. We have a built-in longing to feel accepted and valued. Unfortunately, there are no perfect humans. No one can fully give us what we need. Even if we have dysfunctional families that do not honor and appreciate us, we nevertheless have the perfect Father who will provide everything we need. He's our comfort, our emotional fulfillment, our source of value and affirmation. He honors and celebrates us. In fact, He so lavishes His love on us that we need supernatural help to receive it! Without His help, we can't handle the amount of love He wants to give.

It's natural to feel hurt when people don't value you, say something nasty, or neglect to honor you for who you are or what you've accomplished. It's especially normal to want love and approval from family, and it's wonderful when we receive them. But we won't always receive them. Jesus didn't; His own brothers didn't accept who He was during His earthly ministry (John 7:5). He understands how this works; He knows our need.

I've been in situations in which I wanted to talk about the good things I was doing so people I loved would validate me and think well of me. Getting approval from others is very tempting. We thrive on affirmation. But the moment I start doing that, I can sense they begin to feel as if I'm judging them for not responding the way I think they ought to respond. Then the expectations on both sides begin to escalate, and it feels awful. Or they misinterpret what I say and begin to feel as if I want to boast to make them feel bad. The truth is that we can't get the affirmation we truly need from the people around us. We need to let go of the expectations we've placed on them.

Where do we get it? You can say, "Lord, I have a deep need for acceptance and affirmation. So I bring all I need to You, and I will wait on You to fill me up until I overflow." Because God created us with these needs, and because Jesus can identify with the rejection we often feel and the injustices we've experienced, He welcomes this request from us. He wants to fully dress us in His love before we go out and try to get what we need from other people. In fact, He is jealous to provide this for us. When we go to other people expecting them to feed our need for affirmation, the Spirit is saying, "I really wanted to provide that for you!" And what He wants to give is far better than what the most wonderful human being could provide for us.

When we get what we need from Him, we are free to love others and forgive them of their debts. We can receive whatever affirmation they give, but we don't depend on it. We can absorb rejection and even betrayal, if necessary. Why? Because we've found our home in Christ. We are seated in heavenly places and are filled with the fullness of God. So we are free to let go of expectations and love others as God loves them.

When we walk in this kind of love, we are walking in a greater power than we've ever experienced before. We are free to love spouses, children, parents, friends, work associates, church members, and everyone else the way we were meant to, and they are free to receive love from us. When we are healed from the woundedness that made us needy for affirmation, we are able to offer healing to others. Our need for affirmation and validation will never go away, but God continues to fill it. And we are able to love others into His fullness too.

FREE FOR WORSHIP AND POWER

Like Joseph, David, and many of the prophets, Paul and Silas also experienced injustice. As they were ministering in the streets of Philippi, a slave girl kept following them and crying out about these servants of God (Acts 16). What she said was essentially true, but the spirit in which she was saying it was not a good one. After many days, Paul finally got annoyed enough to turn around and command the spirit to come out of her. She was immediately delivered.

The girl's new freedom made her masters very angry because they had been making lots of money on her fortune-telling abilities. Now those abilities were gone. So they dragged Paul and Silas to the magistrates of the city and leveled charges against them. The residents of many Roman cities were already suspicious of Eastern religions such as Judaism, as many people thought the Jews' refusal to honor Greco-Roman gods and Caesar as a god would bring bad fortune on them. So it wasn't difficult for the girl's masters to stir up animosity toward Paul and Silas and peg them as troublemakers. The crowds and the magistrates had no problem going along with the accusation, so they beat Paul and Silas with rods and put them in stocks in the prison.

They did nothing wrong. Yet these two men were severely beaten with bone-crushing rods and then put in stocks that were designed not only for security but also for discomfort—simply for setting a slave girl free from demonic possession! Not only was that an enormous injustice from a human point of view, but Paul and Silas also could have felt very offended that God allowed this to happen while they were serving Him. In that situation, many of us might have felt abandoned and wondered why we were being punished. It would have been very easy to entertain thoughts of self-pity.

But Paul and Silas didn't go there in their minds, and I love what happened next. At midnight they were praying and singing hymns to God, and the other prisoners were listening to them. They had to have been in great pain physically, and they could have let themselves mentally dwell on the injustice. But they didn't. They sang praises to God, loudly enough for others to listen in.

When we're in a really bad place, it's easy to retreat and do something entertaining or pleasurable to relieve our pain. We watch a movie to forget about our troubles, go shopping to make ourselves feel better, call a friend to complain, sleep long hours, numb ourselves with pleasure (in potentially harmful or addicting ways), or do any number of other things to distract ourselves. And if we don't soothe ourselves that way, we are tempted with all sorts of angry thoughts toward those who hurt us or even accusing thoughts toward the God who let it happen. But God is saying, "I want you to begin to sing! I want you to lift up your voice in praise and worship." When we do that, our spirits begin to rise up and soar.

We miss out on so much from God when we conform to the patterns of the world. The world reacts to injustice with anger and bitterness. It cultivates a mind-set of victimhood, validating our right to be offended for as long as we want. And while it is important to address injustices in society, reacting to them personally by hanging on to a grudge does not help anyone, least of all ourselves. We end up with a lot of patchwork coping skills that really aren't effective at helping us cope at all.

God didn't create us to lick our wounds and feel sorry for ourselves. He did not create us for self-pity and anger; He created us for absolute joy. He has joy for us in the midst of every situation we will ever face. We may have to contend for it, but it's available. If Paul and Silas could find it after having been unfairly and severely beaten, unceremoniously cast into prison, and surrounded by other prisoners, we can find it in our situations too.

Notice how God responded to Paul's and Silas's praises:

> Suddenly there was a great earthquake, so that the foundations of the prison were shaken. And immediately all the doors were opened and everyone's shackles were loosened. When the jailer awoke and saw the prison doors open, he drew his sword and would have killed himself, supposing that the prisoners had escaped. But Paul shouted, "Do not harm yourself, for we are all here."
>
> He called for lights and rushed in, trembling, and fell down before Paul and Silas. He then led them out and asked, "Sirs, what must I do to be saved?"
>
> They said, "Believe in the Lord Jesus Christ, and you and your household will be saved."
>
> —ACTS 16:26–31, MEV

God didn't just set His servants free. He broke everyone's chains. All the prisoners were set free. And at that point, everyone could have escaped unharmed. It looked like a God-given opportunity to run away and never look back. But the jailer was about to kill himself, because that would have been a much better fate than having the Roman authorities hold him responsible for escaped convicts. His supervisors likely would have executed him much more painfully. So Paul told him not to harm himself, because everyone was still there.

Isn't that just like the heart of God? Rather than running from the situation and being free—as they should have been all along—Paul and Silas stayed to help a man in crisis. They could have called him rotten names for overseeing their imprisonment, but they loved on him. He asked how he might be saved, probably thinking of the fate that awaited him in the hands of Roman magistrates. It was a very practical question. But Paul gave him a very spiritual answer, and a more lasting and important one. He told him to believe in Jesus, and then he spoke the word to the man's entire household, and they were baptized. That wouldn't have happened if Paul and Silas had never been imprisoned. The jailer likely would never have met them or heard about Jesus. The enemy's plan backfired. He had stirred up crowds to shut up Paul and Silas, but God took what the enemy meant for evil and used it for good.

> *"Preaching is sowing, prayer is watering, but praise is the harvest." —Charles Spurgeon*

Even if Paul and Silas had been common travelers without any status, their wrongful treatment was unjustified. But their Roman citizenship, which they revealed the next day, terrified the magistrates. It was highly illegal to beat Roman citizens, and Philippi could have lost many of its privileges as a Roman colony on a technicality like that. The magistrates could have lost their position and faced severe punishment for how brutally they had handled Paul and Silas the day before. They pleaded with Paul and Silas to leave in peace. But Paul wouldn't let this injustice fade away in secrecy. He confronted the magistrates and insisted on spending some time with the new church in Philippi before they left.

That is a great story. That's what it looks like to be "more than conquerors." The enemy meant to discourage Paul and Silas and even silence them. God gave them hope, and they could not remain silent at all. I don't know what would have happened if Paul and Silas had slept through the night or pitied themselves while they were imprisoned, but I don't think the story would have ended with an earthquake and marvelous testimonies. They chose to sing in the middle of the darkness, and God responded in power. Wonders followed the praise.

Charles Spurgeon said, "Preaching is sowing, prayer is watering, but praise is the harvest."[1] That's a great statement. God wants to release that kind of praise through you. Whatever you're going through, begin to lift up your voice and sing. Declare His goodness; thank Him for who He is; praise Him for what He is doing, whatever it happens to be. Bless His name at all times in every situation.

I know from experience that it's possible to worship your way out of misery. I've done it many times before. You can become miserable if you choose to just accept your lot in life and try to cope however you can. But no amount of sleep, pleasure, drinking, or distraction is going to get you out of your misery. Worship and thanksgiving will. They work.

Paul and Silas could have grumbled about how they were Roman citizens and how unjust the situation was. They could have been talking loudly at midnight about how they weren't even supposed to be there and how they hadn't done anything wrong. They could have patted themselves on the back for how right they were to set the slave girl free from demonic oppression. They could have filled their minds and mouths with righteous indignation, and they would not have been wrong. But that is a temptation of the enemy, even when it's true. Instead of whining and complaining about the unfairness of it all, or talking ad nauseam about the details of their case, Paul and Silas chose to thank God for what He was doing in the situation, *even though they didn't know what it was.* They had no idea an earthquake and several salvations were forthcoming. They just knew the character of God, and they praised Him.

A BLESSING TO THOSE AROUND YOU

I share often about how I get into situations that prompt me to write speeches in my head. It always comes down to those expectations we talked about earlier—the "shoulds" that eventually lead to judgment. I mull over what I really should say to so-and-so to address whatever offense happens to have riled me up. I want the offenders to hear what they need to hear. I'll go to sleep writing that speech and wake up the next morning adding to it. The problem is that once the speech is written, I'll have to write it again the next night, and the next and the next. That's what holding on to a grudge is like. Instead of letting God fill your heart with dreams and desires, you fill it instead with restlessness and offenses. That's a far cry from peace and joy.

Loving God with all your heart, all your mind, and all your soul looks different from that. When you fill your mind with thoughts that are false and dishonoring to God (Phil. 4:8), you're actually robbing God of the love He deserves from you. Instead of seeking vengeance for yourself, whether in actual practice or in your mind, let it all go. Surrender it to God and choose worship and gratitude instead. Thank Him for His goodness. Tell Him that your purpose on this day and all others is to love Him because He is worthy. Remember that you've been set free, and choose to live in that freedom. He has made a way for your perfect peace. Receive it.

If you can't enjoy God when circumstances aren't quite right, you may never be able to enjoy Him at all, because circumstances are never perfect. Worse yet, you will prove to be an effective tool of the enemy. He will recognize that adversity works in your life; it gets your focus off God and onto yourself and your circumstances. He'll keep trying that strategy until it stops working.

But if you're unmoved—if, like Paul and Silas, you say, "No, I'm not even going to entertain those thoughts; I'm going to sing praises to God"—the devil has little else to attack you with. If adversity brings out praises, which the enemy hates to hear, what else is he going to throw at you? It must frustrate the enemy when adversity produces songs of praise to God!

Nothing in God's Word urges you to waste time and energy on the injustices you've suffered. You're called to stand up for justice in society, but personal offenses are a drain on your true calling. You are free to look for opportunities to minister, release the love of God, and know that your divine purpose is to love God and enjoy Him forever. He has called you to be His friend. You live for fellowship with Him, not for fellowship with unhealthy thoughts. And when you spend time enjoying God presence, the "suddenlies" of God's wonders begin to come. Your praise provokes a season of reaping.

As you begin to thank God for what you haven't yet seen and praise Him for who He is and what He is doing, He releases divine hope to you. That hope becomes a catalyst for breakthrough, and that breakthrough will not benefit you alone. It will benefit everyone around you, just as the earthquake benefited many around Paul and Silas. You have influence through your worship. You may not think so, but it's there. People are watching, and they will see your faith and God's response.

Once when I was travelling, my friends needed to meet me at the border to help me. But as they got ready to leave they realized they had misplaced one of their passports. After a thorough search, they called their mother to pray. And then they danced. In their tiny apartment, these missionaries danced and sang for joy, giving thanks to God for showing them where their passport was even though in the natural it was nowhere to be found. As they were dancing, their mother called and said that the Lord had told her to look under their bed. And sure enough, it was there in a shoebox, and they joyfully headed out to find me. I have never forgotten that story and often do my own happy dances, because I know that sort of faith pleases God.

This is why it's so vital to live with joy and peace. You inevitably affect people around you, whether with discouragement and bitterness or with joy and delight. You can have influence with your complaints or with your praises. It's up to you. But the influence you have with your praise is powerful and lasting. When you start praising and thanking God, it changes the atmosphere around you. It gives people a taste of the kingdom.

Adversity and Works of the Kingdom

Many people are longing to walk in the miracles of God's kingdom. But not many are aware how vital their responses to adversity are in preparing them to walk in the supernatural. A heart filled with praise and thanksgiving can walk in wonders. A heart filled with bitterness can't. Celebration is very often what brings the breakthrough.

I love how Paul and Silas responded to their breakthrough. Not only did everyone get set free, but they had such confidence in God that they stuck around. They recognized He might have a greater purpose for them and their freedom. They would look for someone who needed an expression of God's love.

The enemy will work hard at shutting down your ability to love and minister to others. He hopes that putting you in a bad place will accomplish that goal. So when you're in a bad place, refuse to look inward. Find someone to share the gospel with. Reach out and love. If you start losing your fire, rekindle it by ministering to someone else. That begins to open up the gates of your heart for the river to flow. When you flow out, God flows back into you to fill you up again. Seek first the kingdom of God and His righteousness, and everything else will be added to you. Why? Because your heart is set not on your own situation but on loving God and others.

You've been created for the love, joy, and peace of God's kingdom, even in the midst of adversity and injustice—actually, *especially* in the place of adversity and injustice. If you can become radiant in that place, you will be radiant everywhere. Breakthroughs begin to happen. Circumstances bow to the glory of God. And He steps in with wonders that bless you and everyone around you.

Chapter 6

EXPERIENCING MERCY
OVER THE MESS

W HEN I WAS a teenager, I really wanted to make God happy, so I determined that I was going to pray for an hour every day. Surely that would be a deeply spiritual activity that would please God—my own "hour of power." He can accomplish a lot through an hour of intense praying. So I set about to do that, and after about five minutes, I found myself looking at my watch. I had said all I could think to say. The earth hadn't shaken, and the heavens hadn't moved. What next?

My experience in prayer raised some questions and inspired discussions about all the different ways we can encounter God. I love to pray, and now it is a joy rather than a chore. But do we encounter Him only in intense spiritual activities, or does He speak and move in all the other times of our lives too? Of course the answer is that He speaks in a myriad of ways. We encounter Him by paying attention to Him as a person, not as a one-dimensional being who is available only through specific spiritual disciplines.

He is not an institution but a personality. He has given us power through His Spirit to search Him out, to commune with the Spirit of wisdom and revelation in the knowledge of Him. His Word expresses His thoughts and His ways among human beings throughout all of history, and it tells us how He revealed Himself by becoming one of us and redeeming us. When we feast on His Word, we feast on the thoughts and desires of His Spirit. And all creation declares His glory—in the design of life, in beautiful sunsets and storms, in the vastness of the universe, and more. So we get to experience Him in all sorts of ways.

One of the ways we experience God is by remembering His miracles and marvels and giving Him thanks, as Psalm 103 shows us:

> With my whole heart and with my whole life and with my innermost being, I bow in wonder and love before you, holy God. Yahweh, you are my soul's celebration. How could I ever forget the miracles of kindness you've done for me? You've kissed my heart with your forgiveness and in spite of all I've done, you've healed me inside and out from every disease. You've rescued me from hell and saved my life. You've crowned me with love and mercy and made me a king. You satisfy my every desire with good things. You've supercharged my life so that I soar again like a flying eagle in the sky. You're a God who make things right, giving justice to the defenseless. You revealed to Moses your plans and showed Israel's sons what you could do. You're so kind and tenderhearted to those who don't deserve it, so very patient with people who fail you. Your love is like a flooding river, overflowing its banks with kindness. You will not always be finding fault, never holding a grudge against us, but your mercy overcomes our mess.
>
> —Psalm 103:1–10, TPT

God's mercy overcomes our mess. Isn't that a wonderful statement? Jesus is so magnificent. God has overcome messes in every one of our lives.

I've been on a journey of thanksgiving recently, and the

Word of God encourages me in this. We all know it's good to give thanks, but there is a special delight that comes when you are deliberate about taking time to do it. When you remember the wonders and miracles He has done—and the messes He has overcome—your faith is stirred up. It is set loose to remember how wonderful Jesus is.

When I was first saved, I used to keep a journal of the special things God did for me and the little things He would speak that would touch my heart. It was kind of like my personal history with Him. Every time I would read it, my heart would revisit the gratitude I felt when He first did them, and I'd be reminded of how good and kind He is.

In His parable of the talents, Jesus said more would be given to those who already have. His point was that if we're good stewards of what has been given, we will get more. If we aren't good stewards, even what we have will be taken away. And I always want to put myself in a position of receiving more. That's why it is so important for us to be deliberate in giving thanks to God and remembering His mercies. As we recognize what He is doing, we are stewarding what He has given. If you listen to the stirrings and the leading of God, stewarding what He is giving, He will lead you into greater and greater experiences of Him.

We live next door to a farm. Actually we sort of have a farm ourselves. Tom has four cows, so I jokingly call him Farmer Tom. But next door is a real farm, and a couple of geese from there come across and spend most of their time on our property. There is a white male and a brown female, and they are very cute. They just wander around the yard and peck at the weeds. I get serious delight out of them every morning. Some people might not be excited about intruding geese, but I love watching them. They give me joy. And as I was eating breakfast one morning and watching them, I realized God knows how much I love the geese. He brings them over. So I just had to worship God and thank Him for that little sign of His love.

There is a scene in the film *Amazing Grace* in which William Wilberforce looks at a spiderweb after his conversion and notices just how amazing God is. His beautiful designs are not random and impersonal. They become very personal to the one who notices and is thankful for them. I feel that way when I see a beautiful sunset, as if God orchestrated it just for me! And He orchestrates it for you too, if you notice and thank Him for it. By recognizing that little pull to start giving thanks, you will sense worship begin to well up from inside you. As you worship, God's presence comes in. And you know wonderful things happen in God's presence.

Thanksgiving is not just reserved for the big events, the major breakthroughs God gives us or the problems He solves. It's also for the sunsets and geese and spider webs. These are prompts to worship and praise and give thanks, and God attends to our responses with His wonderful presence.

One night in worship at our church, we seemed to go to an unusually deep place in the Spirit. It was glorious. We worshipped until I could hardly stand up, not because I was tired but because it was just so overwhelming. It was one of those times when we kept pressing in and He kept giving us more of Himself. We experienced His glory. A few mornings later, I was watching the geese again from my window, and I felt prompted to give God thanks. I began singing one of the songs we had sung a few nights before during that wonderful worship service. As soon as I did, the glory came in again. It was overwhelming, and I was overcome with joy—all because I paid attention to a little prompt to give thanks. You see, when we pay attention to what the Spirit is doing, even in something that seems very minor, it blends with what He is showing us in other areas of life. He gives more and more, layer upon layer of His revelation and glory, as we respond to Him.

> *By recognizing that little pull to start giving thanks, you will sense worship begin to well up from inside you.*

When we are faithful to steward our experiences of God, even from the middle of a mess or a wilderness or a dry season, He begins to fill us with hope and peace. Glorious, supernatural encounters are waiting for us, but we can't experience them unless we rise above the mess of our frustration, disappointment, "hope deferred," blind spots, and circumstances. Psalm 103, along with many other passages in Scripture, urges us to get our eyes off our own pain and trials and onto God. Focusing on lack can keep us stuck in it. Focusing on God's goodness—even in the form of geese or a moving worship service—pulls us out of that fruitless place and into deeper experiences of His presence.

TURN YOUR FOCUS OUTWARD

Jonah had some trouble in this area. He was entirely focused on his own situation, and God had to redirect his perspective. It wasn't an easy process.

You may recall from Jonah's story that God called him to go to Nineveh and preach. Nineveh was the capital of Assyria, which was not a very nice nation at all. It had done some particularly brutal things to its enemies, and Israel was one of those enemies. So Jonah had no real love for Nineveh, and when God called him to go there, Jonah ran the other way. God orchestrated a storm, and Jonah admitted the storm was probably a result of his disobedience to God, so he asked his shipmates to throw him overboard. A big fish swallowed Jonah, and God gave him three days in the fish's belly to think about things. He decided God's ways were better, resolved to go to Nineveh as God had commanded, and the fish spat him out.

So Jonah went and preached judgment to the Assyrians. God was going to bring destruction. But to Jonah's dismay, the Ninevites repented, and God withheld His judgment. That wasn't the reaction Jonah was looking for from this dreaded enemy.

But to Jonah this seemed very wrong, and he became angry. He prayed to the LORD, "Isn't this what I said, LORD, when I was still at home? That is what I tried to forestall by fleeing to Tarshish. I knew that you are a gracious and compassionate God, slow to anger and abounding in love, a God who relents from sending calamity. Now, LORD, take away my life, for it is better for me to die than to live."

But the LORD replied, "Is it right for you to be angry?"

Jonah had gone out and sat down at a place east of the city. There he made himself a shelter, sat in its shade and waited to see what would happen to the city. Then the LORD God provided a leafy plant and made it grow up over Jonah to give shade for his head to ease his discomfort, and Jonah was very happy about the plant. But at dawn the next day God provided a worm, which chewed the plant so that it withered. When the sun rose, God provided a scorching east wind, and the sun blazed on Jonah's head so that he grew faint. He wanted to die, and said, "It would be better for me to die than to live."

But God said to Jonah, "Is it right for you to be angry about the plant?"

"It is," he said. "And I'm so angry I wish I were dead."

But the LORD said, "You have been concerned about this plant, though you did not tend it or make it grow. It sprang up overnight and died overnight. And should I not have concern for the great city of Nineveh, in which there are more than a hundred and twenty thousand people who cannot tell their right hand from their left—and also many animals?"

—JONAH 4

In his own mind, Jonah was justifiably angry. This was an enemy who had terrorized his people, and it wasn't fair for them to repent one day and avoid God's judgment for their sins. But God is so much more wonderful than we could ever comprehend. He didn't want to bring destruction on them. He had seen all the evil things they had done. He had watched their children grow up and follow in the patterns that had been set for them. He had sent His angels to watch over them. He knew about all the animals in the city and was concerned for them too. So He did everything He could to rescue them.

The problem was that His prophet didn't see things the way He did. So God showed up not only with compassion for Nineveh but also with an object lesson for Jonah. God grew a vine for shade, which made Jonah happy. Then He took it away, which made Jonah angry. Then He made the point that Jonah's moods were dependent on things he had nothing to do with creating or destroying, and God's plan wasn't really about the prophet's preferences. And if Jonah could get all worked up over a vine, didn't it make sense for God to be concerned for a large city that needed to know Him?

We can get worked up over some of the smallest things. My son recently showed me a YouTube video of people complaining about first-world problems. It really was quite funny: people pouring their cereal and then realizing there was no milk, or lamenting that their iPhone didn't fit into their new skinny jeans. But as God has had me on this journey of thankfulness, I've begun to recognize how many things I take for granted—things I don't deliberately give thanks for. And in not being faithful with what I've been given, I am missing out on the joy that's available through worshipping Him.

I don't ever want to be like Jonah, so absorbed with my own situation that I miss out on the big picture of what God is doing out of His compassion. I want to experience His compassionate, wonderful works. But I'm concerned that this is where many in the church are: waiting for the supernatural to happen but not even noticing the gifts and wonders that are already happening all around them. If the principle is that we receive more of what we are stewarding well, how are we going to step further into the supernatural if we neglect the wonders around us?

Change the Way You Think

When Tom and I first married, we got a little house, and I planted a rose garden outside my window. The first thing I ever planted in that garden was a Mister Lincoln rose, my grandfather's favorite. I watched the bushes grow. A bud eventually appeared, and it grew and began to open up. Every morning I would watch it. Finally, it became a big, full rose. I went outside and cut it, brought it in, and put it in a beautiful vase in my kitchen. It meant so much more to me because I had planted it myself, watched it grow and blossom, and anticipated every day its coming into fullness.

I think this is how God feels about every single person who walks the earth. We tend to think of those around us as just one more person on the planet. We often look at celebrities or politicians as institutions, and we may say things about them we would dare not say to their faces. We'll start throwing rocks at them without spending any time praying for them. But God doesn't do that. He looks at all people as those He cared about before they were formed.

I believe God wants to bring reformation in our thinking. While we're praying and singing about wanting to know God's heart and go deeper with Him, He says, "Actually, I love the ones you don't really like. I love your enemies. I've watched them grow, and My heart is that they would know My love and kindness." He knows about evil generations and people following in the footsteps of their fathers. He knows the end from the beginning. He knew all about the Ninevites who made Jonah angry, but He had an opportunity to save that generation—and even its cattle! He cares about everything.

God says He cares about the sparrow and clothes the flowers of the field. How much more does He love each one of us? He cares more deeply than we can comprehend. And He wants to draw us into that same kind of love and compassion. He wants us to notice the people others don't notice and pay attention to the small, miraculous works as well as the big, flashy ones. He wants us to be deliberate in pressing in and listening to His voice so He can show us things we haven't seen before. He doesn't want to leave us where we are; He wants to draw us out into the glory of what His love really looks like.

I've had the opportunity at recent weddings to talk a bit about true love. It isn't the Hollywood idea of finding someone who will make you feel wonderful. True love gives. It lays down its life for another. It isn't self-seeking; it focuses much more on what you can give than on what you can get. We actually enter into the full experience of true love when we release it to others. That's why Scripture tells us that we love because God first loved us (1 John 4:19). When love is lavished on us, even when we don't deserve it, we begin to love. And if our needs are met through that love, we are free to love others without requiring anything in return. People experience God through us; as He is, so are we in this world (1 John 4:17).

This is a wonderful way for God to overcome our messes. If you are reading this book, there's a good chance you are living in a wilderness season and wanting to experience more from God. Maybe you feel mired in a mess, whether it's your own doing or just the way circumstances have worked out. It is so easy in those seasons to look inward or to focus on immediate circumstances—to look at what you're lacking rather than what you have. And one of God's most powerful mechanisms for getting us out of that place is to move our focus from inward to outward.

So God redirects our attention to what He is already doing, what we already have, the wonders He has already put into our lives. He wants us to focus on His compassion and purposes. Just as He redirected Jonah to stop looking at his own small story and lift his eyes to see His huge purpose, God raises our gaze to greater things—but only if we deliberately choose to acknowledge what God is doing, give thanks for every evidence of His goodness, and let our hearts rise out of the mess.

If you are feeling a little down, there are opportunities all around you to notice things God has put in your life to bring you joy. They are ringing like dinner bells drawing your attention to gifts He has given and more joy to be experienced. As you recognize these gifts, let the Spirit lead you into thanksgiving, and from there let Him lead you into joy. As your heart fills with joy, let Him lead you into worship. In that place, you will begin to experience His embrace, and you will receive even more. To him who has, more will be given (Matt. 13:12, 25:29).

It is perfectly acceptable for you to take precious gifts personally, even if they are as general as a sunny day or a beautiful scene. You can receive them as personalized touches from God and rejoice in them. Some people are looking for a deeper truth of the Spirit, but this is actually very profound. It's also very effective. God will draw you out of a self-focused mind-set and into the bliss of recognizing how very blessed you actually are. Begin to give Him thanks for all you see. Thank Him for the reality of His promises, like the fact that you are seated with Christ in heavenly places, or that God's power is made perfect in your weaknesses. That's what Psalm 103 is talking about—not forgetting the amazing blessings of God. This isn't an obligation; it's an invitation to experience Him more tangibly. Don't wait for something supernatural to happen; God is supernatural, and He is available to you right now. Be a steward of what you already have around you, and it will be the entryway into something more.

When I was writing my first book, I wanted to include some testimonies as examples of what I was writing about. I knew there were many miracle testimonies, but it was difficult to recall the specifics of them or even to remember the details of where and when they happened. I had to call people up and ask. And as people reminded me of what God had done, I realized just how many major miracles I had forgotten. Part of that is just how our memory works, but part of it is that the enemy comes in to steal our joy. If God's miraculous works become a blur in our memory, they are much less likely to encourage us when we're looking to Him for a present need. So it was really wonderful to call people and hear that they were still disease-free many years after they received their healing. My heart exploded with joy all over again.

We have to deliberately become good stewards of our memories so we can recall the testimonies of what God has done. We don't want to lose the joy of celebrating what He has done. That is why a culture of gratitude is so important; it's in that place that we walk in joy and renew our strength. We say with confidence, "I will see the goodness of the LORD in the land of the living" (Ps. 27:13).

COMING OUT OF THE MESS

God understands me even when I don't understand myself. Sometimes I ask Him why I'm feeling the way I do, and He'll tell me. He will point out a resentment or a fear. I ask Him what He wants me to do about it, and He leads me to forgive, release it, or whatever else I need to do. Sometimes I'll be praying and can't put my finger on what I'm feeling, so I ask Him what I really want. He smiles and tells me, and I'll go, "Oh yes, You're right! That's it." He knows my deepest desires better than I know them myself.

The enemy is scared of this kind of fellowship, and he continually tries to rob us of it. He undermines our vision so we will not recognize God's invitation into intimacy. He tries to close our ears to those signals that point us to God's gifts so we will not give thanks for them. We need to recognize what's going on and be vigilant to stop and worship.

Sometimes I'll feel a tug to worship or pray, and I'll think how much more sense it would make to do it later that night when I have more time. Then when I go out that night, God tells me what He wanted to tell me earlier, and I realize how much I needed it that morning. His ways are higher than our ways, and it really is best to let Him orchestrate our lives. He knows how to lift us out of the mess and into a place of peace and joy. We don't ever want to miss out on that.

Whatever happens today, I'm going to rejoice and be glad in You. Open my eyes to the blessings that will provoke my thanks.

I once had people over to my house for dinner, and I could feel God calling me to go pray. It was a bit awkward, but the power of God was very strong. We finished dinner, and I told my friends, "I'm sorry, but you'll have to go home now. I have to go and pray." It felt urgent. As I pulled myself aside, God showed me a situation very clearly in a vision. It was about my husband, Tom, who was in Germany at the time and in a particularly tricky and sensitive situation. So I prayed, and the next day when we talked, I told him what I had seen. He said I had perfectly described the street he was on and the situation he was in, and he agreed that the people with him needed prayer right then. God really does know when to nudge us, doesn't He? It may not always be convenient, especially for those of us used to a Western concept of time and schedules. But His ways are good and are just what we need. He has glorious supernatural encounters waiting for us if we are sensitive to His prompting.

So what do you want? Do you want to go on with bits and pieces of peace and joy, occasional glimpses of how God is working while you're still trying to navigate the mess? Or do you want to go for more—for increasing peace and joy that overcomes the mess and lifts you out? Whatever you choose will determine whether you remain frustrated or find fulfillment. Deep down, you know you are made for more; God's Spirit witnesses to your spirit that this life of peace and joy is available. If you let go and let Him conquer you with His love, you will discover that He is the most fruitful person in the world. You get so much more done when you put Him first—when you say, "Whatever happens today, I'm going to rejoice and be glad in You. I'm going to notice the things You are doing. Open my eyes to the blessings that will provoke my thanks."

I believe the Spirit is leading us into a time of revival, where our hearts are opened up and He is doing supernatural surgery. This surgery is a gift from God that will soften our hearts, take off our blinders, and turn our inward focus upward and outward to Him and His compassionate works in this world. It's a beautiful thing. He wants us to see His goodness and kindness, even in the messes of our lives. His mercy overcomes, and we take part in the overcoming by grabbing hold of the blessings and wonders He is already doing. As we see His compassion, He raises our vision beyond ourselves. And as we steward what He shows us, we receive more.

Chapter 7

RECEIVING FROM THE GOD OF ALL COMFORT

AT THE ANGLICAN school I attended as a child, we repeated a blessing at every assembly. Again and again as a schoolgirl, I recited these words: "Now may the grace of the Lord Jesus Christ, the love of God, and the fellowship of the Holy Spirit be with us all this day and evermore. Amen." But it wasn't until years later when I was driving along in the car and listening to an audio Bible that the wording hit me: "the *fellowship* of the Holy Spirit." That phrase from the benediction in 2 Corinthians 13:14 struck me in a totally fresh way.

Most of us understand theoretically that the Holy Spirit wants fellowship with us. It sounds right and true, and we know the Spirit lives in us and gives us strength and power. Theologically we understand Him as God's active presence in our lives. But do we really fellowship with Him? Do we really receive ministry from Him on a moment-by-moment basis? In relational terms, are we really that close?

The Spirit's desire for us is unimaginably strong, and He longs for us to have constant fellowship with Him. He is giving extraordinary grace for us to enter into that fellowship. Not only does He want to minister to us in a myriad of ways, but He also knows how we will need to depend on Him for what He is leading us into.

When we are still immature in our faith, we may be aware of the Spirit without actively pursuing relationship with Him. We know He'll be there when we need Him. But God's heart in having fellowship with us is for something much deeper than us calling Him when we need Him. Our lives are no longer our own; we have been joined with Him. He wants to walk with us, talk with us, dream and desire with us, and do life together with us. In Him we live and move and have our being. He is wooing us into an understanding of what it means to fellowship with Him and be fully aware of His presence.

We desperately need that kind of communion with Him. The Christians in Laodicea thought they were rich and in need of nothing, yet they were spiritually poor, blind, and naked. They thought they were fine. Jesus rebuked them because they didn't know their own need for Him (Rev. 3:14–22). We need to understand that we always are in deep need of God, and there's nothing wrong with claiming our weakness in that area. It's in our weakness that He is strong. Paul even boasted in his weakness, knowing that this is where Christ's strength is made perfect in us (2 Cor. 12:9–10). In other words, when we recognize our need for God and acknowledge it before Him, we can expect Him to step in with His power.

> *The Spirit's desire for us is unimaginably strong, and He longs for us to have constant fellowship with Him.*

This is why God is called our ever-present help in times of need (Ps. 46:1). The Spirit doesn't want to be available just when we think we need Him. He wants to be available then, but the truth is that we need Him all the time. When we begin to understand that, we find Him available not only when we have a problem but even when we just want to talk.

We really need to put those two revelations together. (1) God is available and powerfully present in our times of need. (2) Our "time of need" is all the time! When we realize that, we suddenly start to wonder why we spend so much time trying to get by without Him—as though we need to ration our dependence on Him for unusual situations.

God wants to release us into an activation in which we begin to arise and lay hold of the inheritance we've been given. We are sons and daughters of the Most High God, and part of our inheritance is having His Spirit walking with us moment by moment. He wants to talk with us, ask us questions, and help in every little detail of our lives.

COMING UP FROM THE WILDERNESS

Joseph spent years hidden in a wilderness of preparation. God had given him dreams as a young man, but his dreams made his brothers angry, and they threw him into a pit and then sold him into slavery. He spent years as a slave, then was falsely accused and thrown into prison, where he spent several more years. Your mind can go to all sorts of places when you've had setbacks like that for long seasons with nothing to do but think and talk to God. Joseph certainly had plenty of long conversations with God. He also had plenty of opportunities to get discouraged, lose heart, and turn away. But he didn't. He drew close. His long season of adversity was really a long season of cultivating fellowship with God.

So when Joseph finally got breakthrough and was summoned to interpret Pharaoh's dreams, his immediate reaction was the kind that comes out of that deep fellowship. He had learned not to rely on his own strength but on God's. He told Pharaoh, "It is not in me. God will give Pharaoh a favorable answer" (Gen. 41:16, MEV). Joseph knew that God had opened up this opportunity, so He would certainly show Himself strong.

This is why God wants us to cultivate intimate fellowship with Him in times of wilderness or waiting. We can't arrive at the fulfillment of dreams and desires and say, "OK, Lord, let me get to know You now." We have to learn who He is and how to depend on Him *before* He launches us into a lifestyle of miracles. He doesn't want us to come to Him with a faint hope that perhaps we might have an encounter with Him. He wants us to come with a certain expectation that He will meet us now and in our times of need. In our hearts, we must know that God will minister to us as we minister to Him. We know by faith that we are accepted in Him, and we boldly approach the throne of grace knowing He will not turn us away.

Think about what might have gone through Joseph's mind as Pharaoh explained his dreams. As a former slave and prisoner, he could soon end up back in prison—or worse—if he wasn't able to come up with an interpretation. He could have wondered if God was going to show up— if years of pain and waiting were going to end with yet another setback: an embarrassing incident in Pharaoh's court. He could have seen this moment as his great downfall rather than his great opportunity. But because of the fellowship forged in years of experiences that seemed to go contrary to his dreams, Joseph knew to boldly claim God would come through. He put his reputation on the line and even staked his life on the God who is an ever-present help. He knew that every opportunity God gives comes with an inherent promise that God will accomplish it if we trust His character. Joseph had to have learned this from years of acknowledging that without God, he could do nothing.

We have to have this kind of knowledge of God—not

just knowing about Him, but knowing Him intimately and personally. We get the assurance in this kind of knowing that we are not standing on the outside but are accepted in the Beloved. We don't wonder in our hearts if He might turn away from us and suddenly give us the silent treatment in our time of need. We know He is going to be like the father of the prodigal son, running toward us to wrap His arms around us and do whatever it takes to restore our souls. That's just who He is. And when we come out of the wilderness with that sort of expectation, we are prepared for the seasons of fulfillment He has set before us.

We go through certain processes and experiences in a wilderness time. We go through trials and difficult circumstances. In the absence of knowing fully what God is doing, we begin to ask questions and wonder why He isn't moving like we thought He would. It's during those times that God wants us to recognize that He is more than enough for us—that only He can satisfy, as we've seen. Like the bride in the Song of Songs, we come up from the wilderness leaning on our beloved (Song of Songs 8:5).

I recall a time of complaining to God about all the deep cuts in my life. I felt so needy, with holes that never seemed to get filled. I was really tired of being a needy person, but I could easily imagine a deep, jagged cut in me. As I was bringing this before the Lord, I saw a vision. A big piece came out of heaven that fit my jagged cut exactly. It filled in every place that was missing, down to my deepest wound.

This is exactly what God is looking for. He isn't searching for perfect people who can serve Him out of their strengths. He is looking for people who know they need Him so He can come in with His perfection and fit the places where we are weak. He doesn't want us to come out of the wilderness in a state of independence, fully sufficient in ourselves to go about His business. He wants us to come out of the wilderness leaning on Him.

That makes a lot of sense of your wilderness, doesn't it? You may have wondered why it is so difficult or long. Perhaps you've been frustrated at how weak your wilderness makes you feel or how wounded you think you are. Maybe you're tired of your failures and flaws and are waiting for God to heal them before He can use you. But the wilderness has been exactly what God intends for it to be. It is turning you toward Him and causing you to lean on Him in every situation. It is revealing just how needy and weak you really are. Did you think that was a bad thing? No, it's putting you in exactly the right position to experience His strength on your behalf. You find Him first in the fire and the hard places of life so you know He is always faithful and true. Then you come out leaning on Him with the confidence that He will come through for you.

Knowing vs. Feeling

I've lost confidence before, even in the middle of a conference. And the reason wasn't because God was not coming through. He was doing some wonderful works. A woman whose eardrum had been cut out from cancer had her hearing restored. It was a wonderful healing, and more miracles continued to happen that night. Cataracts disappeared. I saw a cloudy eye clear up as God came into the room. I saw a man's fingers straighten out, and today he plays the guitar. It was really amazing. But instead of going home excited about what God was doing, I was actually quite intimidated. I knew there was another service the next night, and all these people were going to bring their friends. What if I didn't have it in me to do it all again?

The reality is that I didn't have it in me, even on the first night. It was all Him. The Spirit was there the first night, and there was no reason to think He wouldn't be there the second night too. It didn't matter if I couldn't pull another one out of the bag; I hadn't even pulled the first one out of the bag. But on my way home after the first service, I was aware that the miracles had been so amazing that many more would come with desperate needs the next night, and I began to feel the weight of responsibility.

That night I played a recording of one of my heroes, healing evangelist Kathryn Kuhlman, sharing one of her heart-to-heart talks. She was known for seeing incredible miracles—people getting out of wheelchairs and other clearly dramatic healings. And in that talk I was listening to, she shared how she died a thousand deaths every time she walked out on the platform because she knew many people were at the end of their rope, waiting for God to do something big. I could so relate to that fear, and I was encouraged when she explained how she dealt with that anxiety. She would remind herself that Jesus did everything on earth as a man utterly dependent on the Holy Spirit. "The Holy Spirit never let Him down," she said. "And He will never let *you* down."[1] That word couldn't have been timelier.

The next night I saw another deaf ear open, and the next night another. Since that time, I've seen God do these things so often I wouldn't have room to record them all in a book. And now it seems that everywhere I go, deaf ears open, almost as a regular reminder to me of the lesson I learned that night. People now regularly travel great distances with terminal illnesses to be healed, and I rejoice, knowing the Holy Spirit is so faithful. My spiritual sons and daughters are seeing these miracles firsthand and replicating them all over the world. More and more amazing testimonies are coming in, and it has been a delightful journey. But I know well that this is not about my doing miracles. I have learned from experience that it is all about the Holy Spirit loving people through me, and He can always be trusted to do that in glorious ways.

I often minister to people who tell me they don't feel anything when they worship. They don't feel the intimacy with the Lord they think they ought to have. They wonder when they will get to experience the deep fellowship I'm talking about.

Worship is not about waiting to feel something. The fellowship I'm talking about is not a mood. We may not come up out of the wilderness feeling as though the Lord is our strength. We just have to know that He is. It's a matter of exercising faith in the expectation that God is right there ready to receive us into His arms. He says to come boldly to the throne of grace. He doesn't say we will *feel* bold. He says to *come* boldly.

When you have expectant faith in who God says He is, you can hear His invitation regardless of how you feel at the moment. You know you were in His thoughts when He endured the Cross for the joy set before Him. You are one of His joys. He calls you to come boldly into the fellowship He has prepared for you. There is nothing separating you from Him when you believe in the blood of Jesus. If you confess your sins, He is faithful to forgive them and cleanse you of all unrighteousness. You become the righteousness of God in Christ, and there's nothing that can separate you from His love.

Were you cranky earlier in the day? That doesn't separate you from Him. Did you make the same mistake you made yesterday and the day before? That doesn't separate you either. If you come to Him acknowledging your weakness and sin, He delights to give you strength and mercy. These are rock-solid promises from His Word, whether you feel they apply to you right now or not. His faithfulness does not depend on your mood.

God knows us better than we know ourselves. He is never disillusioned with us, because He knew what we were like before He called us. We are used to human relationships, where when someone is offended it takes a bit of repair work to restore the fellowship. We often have to work our way back into someone's favor when we upset them, don't we? Or at least wait a while until the sting of the offense has faded. But that isn't how it is with God. If He were really offended with us or withholding His favor until we repaired the relationship, no one would ever have an intimate relationship with Him. He would always be offended, because we are always falling short. But He isn't. God knows what we're like, and He loves us. Jesus gave His life because we could never measure up to the standard. He made us new creations and invited us to live in His strength rather than our own. He forgives and invites us to come to Him.

So we don't have to *feel* fellowship with God; we have to recognize it in everything we go through. The Holy Spirit wants us to become more and more aware of what it means to fellowship with Him—to talk with Him, hear His voice, realize it's not within us to answer Pharaoh or perform a miracle, and to place our confidence in Him in every situation. It is not our power that does great works. The power of God is available for those who are intimately entwined with Him and recognize that in Him we live and move and have our being. "The people who know their God shall be strong, and carry out great exploits" (Dan. 11:32, NKJV). The Hebrew word for "know" literally means to be intimately acquainted. Those are the ones who will do great works—not because they have just had a powerful encounter with God but because they have grown close to Him in the wildernesses and trials of life.

God knows what we're like, and He loves us.

I realize believers are already joined with Christ and He is always in us and with us. That's a reality. But I'm not talking about theology; I'm talking about experience. Without faith, you cannot access the promises of God, even though He is with you and in you. So the enemy attempts to distract you or lull you to sleep. He doesn't want you to wake up to the spirit of revelation unveiling who Christ is in your heart on a moment-by-moment basis.

I know these things to be true. And if I have a life message, it's this: the Christian life is all about intimacy. The wilderness may feel like a season of God's silence or neglect, but it's really a season when He has pulled you away with Him in order for you to grow deeper in intimacy with each other. It is your opportunity to discover just how faithful He really is. If you learn only one lesson in the wilderness, it has to be this one: *If you come into intimate fellowship with Him, you get everything. He is the only one who can meet all your needs, hopes, and desires.* The Holy Spirit wants to be closer to you and more involved in your life than a best friend or lover. He wants to be your all in all. And this is what the heart of humanity longs for. This is the revelation that opens up everything else in your life.

No wonder Jesus said the greatest commandment is to love the Lord with all your heart, soul, mind, and strength. Our highest call, greatest joy, and ultimate purpose is to minister to God. And no wonder David wrote that his one desire was to dwell in the house of the Lord all the days of his life and to gaze on the Lord's beauty (Ps. 27:4). Or that Paul wrote that God's grace is made perfect in weakness, and he boasted in whatever frustrations opened the way for God to fill his life. These are divine invitations to find the power of God and discover the gift that has been given to you. Don't waste the trials and tribulations of the wilderness. Recognize that in the midst of them, God is offering to show Himself strong in a way that will bring you deep and lasting satisfaction. You can walk on water in the midst of stormy seasons.

THE GOD OF COMFORT

Tom and I are in the process of raising teenagers. It's a wonderful experience, but it's also a challenging one. One night I said to Tom, "Honey, sometimes I feel very ill-equipped for this. I can't figure out the psychology of it all. I don't know what I'm supposed to say and what I'm not. And I really don't like the thought that I could mess it up."

Now realize this was coming out of the mouth of someone who had been preaching the messages of this book—how God wants to be strong in our weakness, and it's really good to be in an entirely dependent position of leaning on Him. I know this is true, and I can preach it anytime. But it's really hard to grasp in the middle of our situations, isn't it? Knowing it is one thing; applying it is another.

Tom graciously preached my own message back to me and reminded me that God wants to help in everything. It doesn't matter whether or not I think *I* can do it. *He* can do it. His ways are higher than our ways. When we ask for help, it's surprising how He moves. He wants us to taste and see how good He is. His desire to help is greater than we can even comprehend.

We go through many situations in which we simply need God's comfort, and it is readily available. He comforts us not just with a nice pat on the shoulder and a reminder that everything will be all right. In many situations His comfort feels like life itself. It is daily bread that feeds us and gives us just what we need. It doesn't matter whether the situation is big or small, urgent or long term. Even if it's a minor irritation, the God of comfort is there to minister.

> Praise be to the God and Father of our Lord Jesus Christ, the Father of compassion and the God of all comfort, who comforts us in all our troubles, so that we can comfort those in any trouble with the comfort we ourselves receive from God.
> —2 CORINTHIANS 1:3–4

He is "the Father of compassion and the God of all comfort." And which troubles does He comfort us in? All of them. He is the Good Shepherd who makes us lie down in green pastures. He doesn't slap us in the face and tell us to sort ourselves out. He wants to comfort us, give us wisdom, and release peace.

What God is saying in this passage Paul wrote to the Corinthians is vital knowledge for us to carry with us in the wilderness. We all go through things. Paul goes on to write about the dangers and pressures he and his coworkers experienced in Asia, so intense that they despaired of life itself. "But this happened," he confidently claims, "that we might not rely on ourselves but on God, who raises the dead" (2 Cor. 1:9). We likely won't experience the same dangers and pressures Paul faced on his mission trips, but we all have things happen that cause great concern. Attacks come. But the reality is that in everything we go through, we can rejoice because God makes everything work together for our good. He wants to give special comfort that helps us to not only survive but also thrive—to shine as we come through the wilderness into the promises He has prepared.

Stephen was stoned for his testimony of Jesus, but before his accusers dragged him out to kill him, they demanded an explanation before the Sanhedrin. As the council listened to Stephen's testimony, his face shone like that of an angel (Acts 6:15). He didn't die just a noble death; he died with joy as the God of all comfort ministered to him. There can hardly be any better evidence that no matter what we go through, we can be happy in it and receive God's peace. We can do that only in the comfort of His Spirit, not by trying to manufacture happiness and peace ourselves. But as we open ourselves to Him, even in extreme circumstances, these are the outcomes of our fellowship with Him.

I've heard it said that if we don't have joyful anticipation of good in a particular area of life, that area is under the influence of a lie. Romans 8:28 assures us that God is working things together for the good of those who love Him. I've had a tendency to second-guess that promise—maybe I'm not really called, or perhaps I don't love Him enough to qualify—but the truth is, we couldn't come to God if He didn't call us. So if you've come, you're called. And your love, as weak as it may be at times, isn't a litmus test for receiving the promise. God isn't asking you for amazing things; He's asking for mustard seeds of faith. Whether you feel like it or not, you are connected to Him in a love relationship, and you are a full heir of all His promises. That means you can live with radical, relentless hope in every area of your life. God's grace and goodness apply to you.

The enemy will do everything he can to keep you from fellowshipping with the God of all comfort. He will try to undermine God's promises in your own mind and heart. He will hit you with condemnation and shame, trying to get you to punish yourself and forget that you are a new creation whose sin has been entirely paid for.

He will throw all sorts of lies at you—we'll talk more about those in the next chapter—but most of them are designed to cause you to forget who you are or whom you belong to. You have to keep coming back to the God who comforts you in the wilderness, who deeply longs to experience full fellowship and joy with your spirit, and who continues to invite you into your inheritance of all He has promised.

A REVELATION OF STRENGTH

Peter and John were used to perform an amazing miracle in Acts 3. They had gone to the gate called Beautiful, and a man who had been crippled since birth was begging there. They looked at him and said they had no silver and gold but would give him what they did have. What did they offer him? Not persuasive words. Not anything that was naturally in them. Not a formula for supernatural living. No, they simply told him to rise and walk in the name of Jesus. It was a visible demonstration of the Spirit's power.

When the crowd started to gather, Peter responded by asking them why they marveled. "Why do you stare at us as if by our own power or godliness we had made this man walk?" (Acts 3:12). He told the crowd not to look at them as if they had the strength to do this great work. He said it was through faith in the name of Jesus, who was crucified and rose again. And like Joseph many centuries before, Peter spoke with absolute confidence that God would come through for him.

God is releasing the gift of faith in increasing measure in our time. He is releasing revelation that He is the faithful one. As you fellowship with the Spirit, you will come to know more and more that it's not anything in you that causes you to bear fruit; it's all from Him. Like

Peter, you won't take any glory for yourself, because you know that without Him you can do nothing. Your fellowship with the Spirit will increase the humility you walk in, which will also increase the power you walk in. The more you humble yourself and recognize His power, the more you depend on Him for everything.

When Tom and I got married, I soon learned that it was important to him to be the provider. It wasn't a matter of pride; something in him got pleasure out of doing things for me. I was in the habit of buying secondhand clothes, but I remember one day soon after we were married, Tom came home and said he'd seen an outfit that I would like in a store window. It wasn't my birthday or a special occasion; he just wanted to buy it for me because he knew I would like it. He didn't feel obligated. He said, "I *get* to do this for you."

I see that as a picture of God's heart on our behalf. He wants to help us. He wants to show us the glory He can reveal through us, to be our ever-present help in times of need. Now that we are one with Him, He wants to show Himself strong for us. But He will not force Himself on us.

He says: "I lay a banqueting table for you in the presence of your enemies. In all your trouble, I have comfort for everything you go through. Your tears are liquid words, and I can read them all. I know the deepest longings of your heart, and I want to comfort you. I want to walk with you, help you, and be strong for you. But you must come to Me knowing your need and your weakness. Come up out of the wilderness leaning on My arm."

Even Jesus refused to rely on His own strength when He was tempted in the wilderness. He did not buy the lie that He would have to take matters into His own hands and do things for Himself. He cast Himself entirely on the voice of God and would not move from it. He fasted and prayed as He relied on the Father. And He came up out of the wilderness leaning on Him.

As you learn to fellowship with the Spirit moment by moment, I believe He will encourage and strengthen you. God is raising up mighty warriors, but He hasn't called you to fight alone. He wants to give you a revelation of your neediness so you can have a revelation of His strength. Everything you do is to be done in His strength through intimacy with Him. If you want to walk in wonders, you will first have to walk in intimacy.

> *God says, "Come up out of the*
> *wilderness leaning on My arm."*

Only when we recognize that we are experiencing less than God wants to do through our lives do we come to Him asking for help. God never called you to get by or to do OK. He called you to be strong and do great exploits. As you lower yourself in humility and dependence—as you come up out of the wilderness leaning on the arms of your Beloved—He will lift you up in strength and power.

Chapter 8

SPEAKING GRACE TO THE MOUNTAIN

*M*Y HUSBAND AND son both got bows and arrows for Christmas one year, and they spent lots of time in the backyard practicing their archery. I even gave it a go and discovered how difficult it is to pull back before launching your shot at the target. As I watched them practice, the Lord really began to speak to me about that process. The bowstring is pulled back farther and farther until there's great tension in it. The archer focuses on where the arrow is pointed, because if it isn't aimed well and released with a steady hand, someone is going to get hurt. Then when it's time to let go of the bowstring, the arrow launches with great acceleration, following the course that was set for it.

I really believe we are in such a time. God is looking for us to be surrendered like an arrow in the archer's hands. He pulls us further and further back, and there can be great tension in that season of preparation. We may be very aware of the tension, but all we can do is rest. He waits until we are very focused on the target before releasing us, but when He does, we accelerate rapidly toward the goal. For many, the season of being pulled back may actually feel like a time of digression. Yet as we surrender to Him and deliberately allow Him to bring us into a time of focus, we can anticipate an acceleration like we've never seen before. And the arrow is going to hit the mark.

Many other prophets in the church have also received words that point to a season of acceleration. We are in a time of open doors and of seeing clearly. If you want to look, God will show you. If you want to go through the door, God will help you. This is a time of divine invitation.

The prophet Zechariah received an invitation to look behind the scenes at a season of acceleration too. What looked to be a day of small things in the natural realm was really, in the supernatural realm, a day of great preparation:

> Then the angel speaking with me responded, "Do you really not know what these are?"
>
> And I said, "No, my lord."
>
> And he said to me: "This is the word of the LORD to Zerubbabel, saying: Not by might nor by power, but by My Spirit, says the LORD of Hosts.
>
> "Who are you, O great mountain? Before Zerubbabel you will be made level ground, and he will bring out the top stone amidst shouting of 'Grace! Grace to *the stone*!'"
>
> Then the word of the LORD came to me, saying: "The hands of Zerubbabel have established the foundation of this house, and they will even complete it. Then you will know that the LORD of Hosts has sent Me to all of you.
>
> "For who has despised the day of small things? These seven will rejoice and see the plumb line in the hand of Zerubbabel. These are the eyes of the LORD, which survey to and fro throughout the earth."
>
> —ZECHARIAH 4:5–10, MEV

The Holy Spirit is speaking on many different levels in this passage, as He often does in prophetic words. This word was targeted specifically to the people the word was released to, but it wasn't targeted *only* to them. There are layers. And I think one of the layers here is the Spirit's speaking about God's plumb line and His desire to bring us into alignment with it. Before God brings us into a time of fulfillment, He has to bring us into a time of alignment.

Don't let that pass by too quickly. Let it sink in. Alignment comes before fulfillment—just as it does with an arrow aiming at a target. What I've learned as my husband, son, and I have been shooting arrows is that when an arrow is no longer straight (they tend to get bent after a while), it doesn't go exactly where you want it to go.

The Lord is looking for us to come into alignment with His Word. The season of acceleration is coming, but before it does, we need to align ourselves with Him so we move in the right direction. That's why Zechariah's vision mentions a plumb line. A plumb line is a measuring tool that ensures walls and vertical supports are standing straight. God invites us to come into alignment so we will hit the mark when we're released.

Let me be clear about what this *doesn't* mean. The first thing many people think about when they hear of plumb lines and alignment is, "I have to try harder." That isn't what God is saying at all. The arrow doesn't have to try hard when it is in the hand of the archer. It doesn't do anything other than rest in his hands and go where it's guided. But we have a mind of our own, and unlike an arrow, we have to choose to rest in the archer's hands.

I love the way this passage brings that out. It's not by might or power but by the Spirit. The great mountain will become a plain, and the capstone—Jesus—will be brought with shouts of "Grace! Grace!"

In this season of divine invitation, coming into alignment with God includes understanding that we cannot accomplish this by our own might or efforts. We come into that place of surrender like the arrow—by lining up with Christ and who He is. And because of the foundation we have as new creations in Christ, we can shout "Grace! Grace!" to our lives and see them come into alignment. There's no way we can straighten ourselves out by our own efforts; the Holy Spirit has to do it. And He brings revelations of Christ as we put our trust in His ability to make us righteous.

Whatever crooked or intimidating thing tries to limit us, we can shout grace to it and straighten it out. I've heard it explained that grace is faith in God's ability to make us righteous, and legalism is faith in our own ability. By the grace of God, it's no longer I who live but Christ who lives in me. He straightens us out. God gives us the righteousness of Christ.

During this season of awakening, the Lord wants to show you things to come. He wants to direct your focus very clearly. But you have to make a choice to focus on what the Lord has done, not on whatever failings and weaknesses you have. As you focus on who Christ is, resting in the place where you are seated with Him in Christ at the right hand of God, you will begin to see what He sees.

I'm concerned that many in the church are walking around half asleep, not fully aware or fully awake to their purpose. Your purpose is to minister to Jesus and follow Him. It isn't complicated. If you're looking for direction and clarity, that's it. There's no need to look here and there for it. The Lord doesn't get mad at you if you do, but He wants you to hit your target. He is looking for straight arrows to launch. He wants you to have precise clarity in your focus.

One of the best ways to do that is to feast on the Word of God. If your goal is to know God and align yourself with Him, that's a Spirit-inspired desire. He wants you to see Him clearly. And feeding on His Word will help you do that. I love to read the Proverbs every day, just to drink in the wisdom God has given us. I'll snack on His Word throughout the day, and our family reads together in the mornings and again in the evenings before bed. I love to memorize verses and chapters. We want the whole counsel of Scripture! I encourage people to read through entire epistles at a time, not just the bits we like. I encourage reading in all sorts of translations many times a day, not to fulfill any legalistic requirement but to recognize that you are fellowshipping with God as you read. It's a vital way to experience Him.

If Jesus is our foundation, our capstone, and our plumb line, there's no better way to align with Him than to dig into the Word written about Him through the inspiration of His Spirit. And we can do so much more than read; we can use the Word to enter into conversation with Him and seek understanding from Him. He wants to give us eyes to see and ears to hear Him well.

SHOUT GRACE TO THE VOICES

The enemy is out to discourage you. I'm sure you've experienced His attempts to do so. He wants to deceive you into seeing God and yourself from a false perspective. I've found that discouraging thoughts are most likely to hit after a victory. Coming down the mountain is sometimes more dangerous than going up. I ask my intercessors to pray just as much after a crusade as they do during the preparation, because I believe you're more vulnerable after a victory than before it. That is when your focus can slip. Your mind and your body cry out for rest—just a little "vegging out"—and you let down your guard. You might watch something that grieves your spirit or second-guess what God has done and begin to lose the joy of it.

It happened with Elijah; he won a huge battle against the priests of Baal, then slipped into deep depression when the king and queen didn't repent as they should have. He was so discouraged that he asked God to let him die (1 Kings 19:4). If that can happen to Elijah, it can happen to us if we aren't careful. We have to recognize there is an enemy, fix our eyes on the Lord, and maintain focus throughout our preparation and launch.

If you are struggling with thoughts of discouragement, take the thoughts captive. With every "should have," "could have," and "would have," thank God for what you were able to do and how He brought you through. I often have these thoughts on Sunday nights after ministry. I think of what I should have said better or worry about who I missed talking to, and I have to recognize what's going on. I recognize there is a fight, just as real as if intruders came into the room and began stealing from me. "No, I'm not going there, devil," I declare. "Holy Spirit, thank You for the words You sent forth, and I declare they will accomplish everything You intend." And I refuse to be discouraged, even when the temptation is great.

Voices will always try to speak to you. They will try to discourage, intimidate, and condemn. The enemy wants to get you to look at the negative and focus on whatever seems to be going wrong—or whatever might possibly go wrong. He wants to bring you into a place of fear, depression, and anxiety. Whatever you've been struggling with, he will try to intensify not only the struggle but also the guilt over it. If you've been fighting an addiction, the voices saying you need it or deserve it will get increasingly louder. You have to recognize there's a war going on, and God has given you power to speak to the mountain. If voices of condemnation or fear have been shouting at you, shout at them even louder. "Grace, grace, in the name of Jesus!" There is power when you open your mouth and let

God's Word go forth. Your mouth is an open door for the King of kings to come in with glory.

Is your heart condemning you?
God is greater than your heart.

Discouragement, fear, and condemnation are not your lot. You don't have to accept them. God says His kingdom is righteousness, peace, and joy in the Holy Spirit (Rom. 14:17). Anything that isn't pure, lovely, or of good report does not belong in your head. You cannot welcome those thoughts.

As you speak against those thoughts, recognize the example Jesus set for us. After forty days in the wilderness without food and water, Jesus was desperately tired and weak. The enemy came with all sorts of temptations to exploit His vulnerability. Jesus didn't spend time weighing whether to entertain His temptations. He didn't rebuke Himself for being tempted. He clearly recognized what was going on and countered with the truth. (See Matthew 4:1–11.)

We are to do the same. It isn't our job to examine the lies, focus on the negatives, and figure out strategies to deal with feelings such as discouragement, fear, and condemnation. Our job is to release light. If you're trying to bring light into a dark room, you don't try to figure out the darkness. You don't even address the darkness. You simply turn on the light. And when the voice of lies speaks to you, all you have to do is bring the truth. The light of God's Word overcomes darkness. You are never a victim; you're a victor.

If you don't know what to pray, start with the Lord's Prayer, or even with a psalm. Just start. The Word of God is quick and powerful, and it will accomplish what it set forth to do. Pick up the sword of the Spirit and fight. Shout "Grace, grace" to the voices of condemnation and fear.

Recognize what is going on in your heart. Is your heart condemning you? God is greater than your heart (1 John 3:20). The enemy is after your heart because he is terrified of those who know their hearts are free, cleansed by the blood of the Lamb, and righteous before God. Hearts like that come boldly to the throne of grace in times of need. They ask for open doors and are free to walk through them.

GET READY

This is a time of open doors. God's people have the capacity to ask and receive like we've never done before because of the revelation that is being released in this age. We have come to know God deeply, but what we know of Him is still only a tiny fraction of what there is to know. He has so much more in store for us. There will be an increase in revelation knowledge—not just for the sake of our curiosity, but so we can wake up and know His power toward those who believe. He is not preparing us to merely survive the wilderness. He is preparing us to take up our weapons of warfare against strongholds and actually take nations. Compared to what is coming, we've been only in primary school. It's time to get up and start taking land in the Spirit.

One of the greatest areas in which we must align ourselves with God is the area of forgiveness. You may not think of forgiveness as a powerful weapon that pulls down strongholds, but it is. The Scripture passage that talks about how we are not ignorant of Satan's devices (2 Cor. 2:10–11) is about the enemy's ability to sow division among God's people. Forgiveness is a key that helps us undo the enemy's schemes.

To forgive as God forgives us is a big deal. We are called to love one another as God loves us.

Therefore, as God's chosen people, holy and dearly loved, clothe yourselves with compassion, kindness, humility, gentleness and patience. Bear with each other and forgive one another if any of you has a grievance against someone. Forgive as the Lord forgave you. And over all these virtues put on love, which binds them all together in perfect unity.

Let the peace of Christ rule in your hearts, since as members of one body you were called to peace. And be thankful. Let the message of Christ dwell among you richly as you teach and admonish one another with all wisdom through psalms, hymns, and songs from the Spirit, singing to God with gratitude in your hearts. And whatever you do, whether in word or deed, do it all in the name of the Lord Jesus, giving thanks to God the Father through him.

—COLOSSIANS 3:12–17

This is a good passage to memorize; it's a great description of what it means to follow Jesus. Receiving God's love and forgiveness is beautiful and life changing, but receiving is not our only responsibility. God wants us to receive and then give to others from what He has given us. That's why Paul writes, "Forgive as the Lord forgave you." There are very practical aspects of manifesting God's love. He makes His face shine on us so we can shine on everyone around us. I look at people with an awareness of the reality of Christ in me, aware that I have access to His thoughts about them. I pray, "Come on, Jesus. Shine! Let them see You in my eyes." I want people to be blessed, to encounter God's love in my every handshake, greeting, or smile.

That's what Paul is writing about in Colossians—that people would feel the presence and love of God in us, simply by being around us. When believers gather together, the love should be tangible and overflowing. We should walk around with psalms, praises, and thanksgiving in our hearts. We must be deliberate expressions of God's peace, wholeness, and fullness. That's what life in Christ is meant to look like—righteousness, peace, and joy in the Spirit.

But it's so easy for us to be drawn into deception instead. The enemy is more crooked than you can imagine. He's like the worst kind of trial lawyer trying to distract from the real issues with legalistic technicalities. He is out to trap you with a sense of human justice that doesn't take God's grace into account. Don't let him get away with that. Don't waste time looking to the prosecutor. Look to the judge.

My own sense of justice used to convince me to deprive people of grace. If they had done something wrong and wouldn't acknowledge that it was wrong, wouldn't my grace be an injustice to them? How would they ever learn how wrong they were if I just forgave them and they never realized what they did was wrong? I would forgive them, of course, but I wanted them to know that what they did needed to be forgiven. And I'd let them know with my icy body language.

That's not true forgiveness. God tells us to forgive others in the same way He has forgiven us, and that isn't how He forgave us. We will never hear Him say, "Well, I forgive you, but I'm going to hold it over your head until you learn a lesson." God's voice never sounds like that.

Think about how Jesus forgave. He had been beaten, bruised, whipped, bloodied, and marred beyond recognition. He took everyone's sins on Himself. He hung on a cross as people jeered, cursed, and spat at Him. This was history's greatest injustice, the only perfectly innocent person being brutally executed like a hated criminal. And as they crucified Him, He looked with compassion at them and said, "Father, forgive them, for they do not know what they are doing" (Luke 23:34). He wasn't saying, "Father, hold this over their heads until they repent, and then forgive them." He was crying out that they be forgiven before they ever acknowledged they had sinned. He offers the forgiveness, and whether or not we receive it and engage in the divine exchange of receiving righteousness for our filthy rags is up to us. He loved us first, and it is His goodness and kindness that leads us to repentance.

Jesus did the same with the woman caught in adultery (John 8:1–11). He offered forgiveness to her before she said a word. She hadn't apologized or pleaded for mercy. Neither had the man who was lowered through the roof by his friends in order to be healed (Mark 2:1–11). Yet the first thing Jesus said to him was a declaration of forgiveness. This seems to be a pattern with Him, doesn't it? We reserve our forgiveness until we hear an apology, and that sends us off into judgment, fear, and a fight we were never called to be in. Jesus never went there. He forgave. And God's Word tells us to forgive in exactly the same way.

You can trust God with other people's sins against you. If you let them go, He will have His way. His response may not look like your sense of justice, but it will be right. He declares that vengeance is His, so if vengeance is warranted, He will take care of it. But God's preferred form of justice looks like a Savior on a cross. We're very glad to apply that sacrifice to ourselves and claim the freedom He offers. But we can't apply it to ourselves without also applying it to others. The need to have closure by seeing someone else pay for their offenses against you will keep you in an emotional prison.

If you really want to walk in wonders, learning to forgive is a critical part of your preparation process. So many people want God's miracles without understanding His compassion or character. Jesus was moved with compassion and healed people. Faith works by love. Without an intimate understanding of God's heart and an awakening of His heart in us for people, the flow of power will be limited. Ministry is a manifestation of love. Without an awareness of how much we have been forgiven, we forget the power of forgiveness.

> *You can trust God with other people's sins against you. If you let them go, He will have His way.*

Here's what God's forgiveness actually looks like:

> The Lord your God is in the midst of you, a Mighty One, a Savior [Who saves]! He will rejoice over you with joy; He will rest [in silent satisfaction] and in His love He will be silent and make no mention [of past sins, or even recall them]; He will exult over you with singing.
> —ZEPHANIAH 3:17, AMP

God has removed our transgressions from us as far as the east is from the west (Ps. 103:12). It is the kindness of God that leads to repentance (Rom. 2:4). The message of the gospel is that Jesus has already forgiven your sins and is waiting for you to respond and receive Him and His mercy. He has already made a way for you to come into relationship with Him and receive forgiveness of sins. That is the message that causes hearts to melt and repent. None of us come to God with gratitude that He is holding sins over our heads until we can repent hard enough. No, our hearts are filled with praise and thanks because He is no longer holding sins over our heads and invites us into new life.

That means it is never our job to focus on the negative and try to shovel the darkness out of anyone's life. We bring the light, and light dispels darkness. Jesus shows us how to do that by forgiving those who don't deserve it and who may not have acknowledged their sin. As we release undeserved forgiveness, we release the power of God's goodness. And that power manifests in ways that go much further than forgiveness. Shouting grace to our situations and speaking it into the lives of people who need it prepares the way for the miraculous.

WALKING IN JOY, WALKING IN POWER

As I shared earlier, I've struggled so much in the past with this issue of forgiving people who have wronged me. I used to write scripts in my head and then play the video of my speeches—you know, the perfect words that would force them to see things my way and realize how wrong they had been. I'd fill my brain with the right retorts or convincing arguments, and there wouldn't be much room for what the Spirit wanted to speak to me prophetically. That kind of thinking takes precious time and brainpower that the Spirit wants to use for other purposes. We've been created for fellowship with Christ, and every moment we spend dwelling on something that isn't pure, lovely, or of good report robs Jesus of the joy that was set before Him.

Focus on the goodness of God—to know it for yourself, but also to release it to others. If you're trying to get someone to repent or apologize to you, then you're focusing on the negative. Let it go. Release God's goodness to that person, whether or not he or she is deserving or even aware. Whatever it takes, learn to walk in joy.

I'm so glad I don't have to live with anyone who is miserable. But if you've ever spent much time around someone who has no joy, it isn't very pleasant, is it? People want to be with you when you're happy. If you're miserable, you actually rob the people around you of the joy they could experience. Your freedom and joy are certainly beneficial to you, but they are also vital to the people around you.

When you and the people with you are free and happy, you can dream together. Instead of focusing on fixing whatever problem you're facing, you can enjoy one another's company and begin to make plans about your hopes and dreams. Believe it or not, this is what God is looking for every day with you. He has been looking forward to fellowship with you from before the foundation of the earth. That's what His sacrifice was about—bringing us into new life and freedom so He could have face-to-face fellowship with us. He wants to fill you with His dreams and desires so His glory will cover the earth through His people. In a place of intimacy with God, His people know Him deeply and are empowered to do great exploits that reveal His kingdom on earth. That is God's purpose, and it's available right now.

Be aware that there is a war going on in your thought life. Voices are shouting at you and trying to burden you with discouragement, fear, and condemnation. An unforgiving attitude is trying to shackle you and prevent God's power and goodness from flowing through you. The enemy comes and reminds you of how people have offended you, provokes fear that they are talking about you, and convinces you that they are hostile to you. He exploits divisions and puts up strongholds.

You have everything you need to undo them. Lay hold of the truth that repairs divisions and pulls down strongholds. Shout "Grace! Grace!" to your situations and to the people around you. Lift up to God every discouraging, fearful, condemning thought and every injustice you experience. Refuse to be imprisoned by these things by releasing them to God and choosing instead to walk in joy.

As you lift up your grievances and concerns to God, the question of why, when, and how long will begin to fade away. Speak grace, and the power of the Word will accomplish what you send it forth to do, because it's God's Word. It will not return to Him void. You have power that you have not even begun to tap into, but you can begin now. Get up and pray, speak, and declare grace. Look with joy and expectation at the goodness of God that will manifest in your life and the lives of those around you.

Become a straight arrow fully focused on the target and at rest in God's hands. And when you are ready to launch, you will fulfill your purpose exactly as God designed you to do.

Chapter 9

PRAISING IN THE STORM

I'M A STORM watcher, and one of our recent storms was spectacular. God put on a show. Our family sat on the porch and listened to the storm all evening. And because I'm a music teacher and I love to sing, we sang. We sang hymns, songs from musicals, and whatever else came to mind. Later the storm turned around and came back, with lightning painting the sky. It was magnificent. We sang some more and got creative with our harmonies, and I'm pretty sure some angels bent low to listen.

One of the songs we sang was a familiar hymn: "When peace, like a river, attendeth my way, when sorrows like sea billows roll; whatever my lot, Thou hast taught me to say, it is well, it is well with my soul."[1] When I went to bed later that night, I heard the Lord speak to me. He told me these weren't random songs coming to our minds. The ones we chose had meaning.

I've been trying to develop ears to listen to what God is saying, because all too often we miss His voice. So I thought through which songs we had sung, some of them seemingly meaningless at the time: "Tomorrow" from *Annie*, "The Impossible Dream" from *Man of La Mancha*, and several others that seemed perfectly designed to release hope for the future. God spoke to me about His desire to bring hope. That's why we can sing "It Is Well"; whatever our lot is, we know in our hearts God wants to release hope.

Horatio Spafford, the man who wrote "It Is Well With My Soul," had experienced a series of tragedies in his life.

His son died at the age of four; he lost much of his business in the Great Chicago Fire; and then when his wife and four daughters were traveling to Europe, the ship they were on collided with another and sank. All four daughters died. He wrote the hymn as he was traveling to Europe to be reunited with his wife and passed the spot where the ship had sunk.[2] "When sorrows like sea billows roll" was not just a poetic phrase for him; it was a heartbreaking reality.

> *Your destiny is to be a friend of God, to stand in His counsel and hear His heart.*

The truth is that whatever you're going through, God's desire is to fill your heart with love, peace, and hope for the future. Whenever you face adversity, it is very tempting to turn your prayers into worries rather than expectant hopes. You end up praying not in faith but in anxiety, pleading with God to do something, not getting excited in your heart about what He is going to do. God wants to release you into hope so you can begin to celebrate.

Even when we're hurting, God wants to impart peace into our souls so we can say, "It is well," knowing that with Him, it really is. We are to be people who are not undone by adversity. In fact, we can thrive in it.

Something happens when you get deliberate and begin to set your eyes on God in the midst of a storm. When you let the Holy Spirit lift up your head to see Him above everything else, you begin to delight in Him. His joy becomes your strength. He empowers you to not only survive but also to go out and be a blessing.

The Lord reminded me of what I really desire as I was talking with Him recently—my deepest, truest desires. The Bible tells us that as we delight ourselves in Him, He gives us the desires of our hearts. Sometimes my mind gets cluttered with things I want to happen—breakthrough in this person's life, salvation for another one, and other things that would be great to see happen. But I can actually get consumed with these things. God reminded me that my greatest desire is to love and enjoy Him, and I thought, "Oh yes, that's right." In the midst of our longings to see things happen, we can actually miss our highest calling. But this is our deepest joy, the thing we long for more than anything else. Just to be connected to Him and minister to Him is the greatest calling we have. We were created in His image just for fellowship with Him. That is our purpose.

If you're ever desperate for a prophetic word, take that one. Your destiny is to be a friend of God, to stand in His counsel and hear His heart. You may feel like surviving is all you can do, but to actually be a friend of God on earth and talk with Him is so much more significant than just getting by. You were created to love Him and be loved by Him. One of your greatest responsibilities is to let Him lavish love on you. Can you imagine that? It isn't hard work. He wants to give you His Spirit so He can strengthen you supernaturally to comprehend how amazing His love for you is and be able to handle it when He pours it out on you.

There is absolute joy in God's presence. But as you know, you go through plenty of seasons of life that are not absolute joy. It isn't that God's presence has left; the problem is that it's hard to sense His presence when we go through dry times or face adversity. And during those times, a tempter comes along and tries to fill our mind, heart, and soul with things that distract—offenses that get us worked up inside thinking of how to respond; worries that turn our focus to circumstances; pain that we swallow rather than sowing back to God for a blessing. The enemy tries numerous ways to separate us from the experience of God's love and joy.

MINDS FULL OF PRAISE

God wants us to love and worship Him at every level of our being. That is the heart of the greatest commandment:

> One of the teachers of the law came and heard them debating. Noticing that Jesus had given them a good answer, he asked him, "Of all the commandments, which is the most important?"
>
> "The most important one," answered Jesus, "is this: 'Hear, O Israel: The Lord our God, the Lord is one. Love the Lord your God with all your heart and with all your soul and with all your mind and with all your strength.' The second is this: 'Love your neighbor as yourself.' There is no commandment greater than these."
>
> —MARK 12:28–31

The Lord has been speaking to me about what it really means to love Him with my mind. We often hear things like "Let go and let God," or "I'm too much in my mind." I understand the intent—that God isn't looking for us to analyze everything and figure it out. Sometimes we really should apply the thoughts in Psalm 131:1: "I do not concern myself with great matters or things too wonderful for me." We should just rest in the arms of God when we encounter things we don't understand. But God also gave us a mind. We couldn't switch our brains off if we tried. He likes us the way we are. He wants to engage with us in our thoughts.

Imagine being in any other relationship and trying to switch off your mind. How would you get to know the other person? Relationships don't develop passively. So if we're in a relationship with God, we have to be able to worship Him fully engaged in our minds, as well as our hearts and souls. As we come before the Lord, He helps us fix our minds on things above (Col. 3:1) and on things that are pure, lovely, and of good report (Phil. 4:8). When our focus is set on Him, we are filled with His joy, kept in perfect peace, and walking in His love. So God wants us to be very deliberate about fixing our thoughts on Him in worship.

We see this very dramatically in the story of Paul and Silas in Philippi that we looked at in chapter 5. A young woman possessed by a spirit had been following them and shouting, creating quite a distraction. Finally Paul came to the end of his patience, turned around, and commanded the demon to leave in the name of Jesus. She was freed, but her masters got very upset, as she had been a huge source of income for them. So they dragged Paul and Silas before the magistrates, where they were brutally beaten with rods and thrown into prison.

So Paul and Silas, very much in pain from their beating, spent the night in jail surrounded by other prisoners. We would consider their situation to be extreme adversity, but Paul and Silas didn't lament their circumstances. Their unexpected response was to worship, singing psalms and hymns loudly enough for others to hear.

Later on when Paul writes to rejoice in everything or to give thanks in everything, we know the kind of experiences he includes in those instructions. He applies those words even to extreme pain and prison. If he could worship God in those circumstances, he could worship in any kind of storm. So he knows what he is talking about when he says to rejoice. He really does mean for it to apply at all times.

As our family sat outside watching the storms and singing old hymns, I began to think about the words Horatio Spafford penned. They were true. We really should be able to say, "It is well with my soul," whatever the circumstances are. We have hope that others don't have. The Bible tells us that God is working all things together for our good. So we really can claim, "It is well with my soul."

But how can we do that honestly when there is a war going on inside of us? When the enemy tries to fill our thoughts with the negative side of circumstances and all the worries, bitterness, and discouragement that can surround them, how do we turn our minds back to God? We have to be very stubborn about taking every thought captive and worshipping God in the storm. It can begin very simply with "Thank You for Your love for me, Your faithfulness, Your goodness, and Your kindness." Whatever it takes, begin somewhere. Begin to declare the word that He who has purposed it will also do it (Ps. 57:2; 1 Thess. 5:24). Eventually your mind will be filled with the peace and joy of God.

I've found my mind getting crowded with thoughts, answers, and breakthroughs I'd love to see, and I've fallen into the trap of praying my worries. It is so easy to pray and not be happy about what you're praying about. But God wants us to pray with thanks and certain hope that His answer is going to be good, so I've learned not to pray with anxiety anymore. As I lift my prayers to Him, as I pray blessing over people, I ask with joy—even if I'm praying from a place of adversity. I know He is about to do something good in response to my prayers.

What would you find if you took inventory of your thoughts? What goes on in your mind most of the time? Where does your brain go when you're in default mode? The enemy often comes in and plants things in your mind that become your focus, even though you never intended to spend time thinking about them. If you're passive about your thoughts, this can happen a lot. But if there is anything running through your mind that is not Christ alone, the goodness of God, the joy of the kingdom, and all that is pure and true and right, you're missing out on God's fullness. God is looking for you to deliberately set your mind on things above and bless Him.

If you have been wondering when you're going to get your breakthrough—healing for your body, salvation for your family member, answer to your prayer—you have to realize that God wants you to break through on the inside more than He wants you to break through on the outside. He wants you to overcome the adversity in your heart and mind before He overcomes the adversity in your circumstances. Our thoughts can actually rob us of the peace He wants to give us. Thanksgiving and praise restore it to us.

Consider all the thoughts that could have gone through Horatio Spafford's mind (and probably did at one time or another): "How did this happen? Lord, why did You allow this? Am I being punished?" And think about all that might have gone through Paul's and Silas's minds as they sat in prison after being unjustly beaten: "Lord, this isn't fair. We've been serving You. Why are You giving the enemy the upper hand? We should not be suffering like this." In the midst of adversity, we have plenty of opportunities to question, doubt, become bitter, grow discouraged or depressed, and even turn away from God. Our minds will easily take us to all of these places, especially when the enemy infiltrates with his distortions and accusations. And unless we change the subject, this is exactly where our thoughts will go. But whatever circumstance we find ourselves in, God is looking for us to lift up our voices and begin to praise and worship Him.

The enemy is an expert at replaying all the things that have gone wrong in your life or that haven't yet been resolved. It's like he's playing DVDs in your mind. When you're trying to go to sleep, or wake up in the middle of the night, this is what begins to play. "Look at the injustice. There's nothing you can do about it, is there? That was so unfair, so terrible." And he sits there and laughs at how you're being robbed of fellowship with God because of what is filling your mind.

I was going through a difficult time during one of my pregnancies, and as any mother can tell you, hormones amplify every emotion when you're pregnant. I not only felt the weight of everything that seemed to be going wrong; the weight was magnified to the extreme. So I became very discouraged and depressed, and I was certain no one could understand what I was going through.

I really went to the depths. I honestly felt suicidal at times. Of course I knew it wasn't right to commit suicide, that it wouldn't be fair to the family. And realizing there was no way out made me feel even more hopeless! But I learned that when you're in that place, God is there. He's with you. He's not looking to give you sympathy, though He loves you and cares for you deeply. He wants to bring truth.

I was afraid to get alone with my thoughts during that season. I needed distractions, because without them, my thoughts would start to descend into a deep spiral. I was afraid of being alone, but I didn't want to be with people. That's how ugly depression looks. I don't talk about it very often, but the reality is that many people have felt this way, and what I learned in my experience may be helpful. I got to a point where I had to choose whether to live in that deep, dark place or to get up.

I decided it was time to get up, and the only way to do it was to change the channel in my mind. Whenever those thoughts came, I had to replace them with something else. When I went to take a shower or wash the dishes, I would put on some good teaching cassettes—these were the days before digital audio—and listen to truth. I would find places that lent out cassette sermons and listen to everything I could. I needed the channel of God's truth to play in my mind rather than the channel that had been playing. No human could help me, though many tried. Tom helped a lot, but he had to go to work every day, and he couldn't do what only God can do. But when we are deliberate about refusing to live in that dark place, God comes through. He wants us to recognize that we are in a battle, pick up the sword of the Spirit, which is the Word of God, and use it. That is when breakthrough starts to come.

I'm in a wonderful place now, and the battle has changed. But that doesn't mean the battle ever stops. They are different in each season of our lives. In every battle, however, the answer is the same. God says, "Lift up your head! I'm putting a sword in your hand, and I want to help you use it. I've made a way of escape for you, and it's time to get up!" Even today I find myself going over negative details in my head and wasting time on things that are not worth my time or thoughts. And I have to be vigilant about replacing those thoughts with God's truth.

You may have thought your wilderness or your adversity was all about you, but it's much bigger than that. Your breakthrough will affect everyone around you.

We need to realize how the enemy is trying to rob us of fellowship with God. There are times when I can feel my mind going toward negative thinking and I can almost hear the enemy whispering, "Come down here." I have to say, "No, I'm not going there." I put a stop to it because God has given us power by His Word to change our focus, to set our minds on things that are good and lovely and true. His Word is designed to bring us life and hope. But we have to be vigilant about declaring the Word over negative thoughts.

Worshipping God with our minds is all about focus. When you are focusing on things that are going wrong, you're missing out on the joy set before you. If you envision any destiny that isn't primarily about loving God and being loved by Him, your focus is off. There may be times when it seems that even God can't sort things out in your life, but His heart is for you to fix your mind on Him and begin to worship and bless Him. The peace that transcends your understanding comes in and takes you to a place where you can pray in freedom and hope. That brings you back to the glorious reality of who He is and who you are in Him.

When Paul and Silas did this, God caused an earthquake that threw the prison doors open and broke the prisoners' chains—not just those of Paul and Silas but of everyone in the prison. Everyone got breakthrough. That is not why Paul and Silas were worshipping God, but it was one of the outcomes. Their praises moved God, and God moved in their circumstances.

As you begin to praise God, not only do your shackles come off, but so do everyone else's. You start to affect the atmosphere around you. You may have thought your wilderness or your adversity was all about you, but it's much bigger than that. Your breakthrough will affect everyone around you.

Have you ever met someone who was really going through a hard time, and when they walked into the room, within ten minutes a lot of people had heard how awful everything is? When people are in pain, they tend to talk about it. And it can be helpful for them to process their thoughts with trusted friends. But that conversation should never go long without some element of hope in it. Some people spread their negative, hopeless thoughts very liberally to a lot of people a lot of the time. They are reflecting what they are beholding. The Bible tells us that as we look at the glory of God, we are transformed to reflect that glory (2 Cor. 3:18). But the opposite is also true; if we stare at our adversity and suffering long enough, we begin to be transformed into its likeness. And that affects everyone around us too.

No one likes to be around those who talk about their problems with no hope. It's not very attractive. "I'm just being real" is often a cover for hopelessness. If you really want to "be real," then reflect the reality that God hasn't created us to live in misery. He has called us to much better things. And instead of allowing our thoughts to be fixed on what's not going well, we need to fix them on the glorious thoughts of having been saved, rescued, restored, redeemed, chosen, equipped, and blessed to minister to the heart of God and the needs of others.

There is no higher calling than this. People who come to a worship service and say they aren't getting much out of it are missing the point. Worship is about fulfilling our destiny to bless the heart of God. You can do that in any service anywhere. And in the process of blessing the heart of God, you come into a place of perfect peace and fullness of joy. Your strength is renewed.

The Bible says that those who look to God are radiant and their faces are never covered in shame (Ps. 34:5). But those who look to their problems are miserable, and their faces are never happy. And we really do have a choice. If anyone had an opportunity, or even a right, to be miserable, it was Paul and Silas after being beaten with rods for setting a girl free and then being thrown into prison. They could have felt sorry for themselves. Horatio Spafford could have been miserable after losing a son to disease, his investments to fire, and four daughters to a shipwreck.[3] But who wants to live in a prison of misery? How long do we want to put up with shackles? We have a choice to look to God and be radiant; to love Him with our entire heart, soul, and mind. We'll have to refuse the invitation to a pity party, but God's invitation is so much more satisfying. It's really glorious.

We have to reject the DVDs the enemy wants to play in our minds. They are not going to help us. We have to reject the temptation to write speeches in response to our injustices and offenses. It is a strong temptation; we want to satisfy our own sense of justice and make sure people know what they did wrong. Something inside us wants to tell them off. But the problem with speech writing is that it never ends. And if you do get to deliver the speech you've spent so much time developing, you're usually sorry you did. I know how this works; I have a lot of experience in internal speech writing. It robs us of joy, and it ends up being a bad idea. God wants us to recognize what's going on inside and accept the invitation to love Him with everything in us.

Our family has been talking about keeping things "shiny white" at home—to feed on whatever is pure, lovely, and good. I have to be careful about the movies we watch and the conversations we have. I need to guard my heart because what goes in is what comes out. What I focus on is what is reflected. I can't afford to have my mind dwell on anything ugly. If it's a little bit gray, we need to stay away.

The Father is looking to help you walk in the freedom He purchased for you. Whatever adversity you're facing, whatever shackles are holding you down, whatever questions have been tormenting your mind, now is the time to be free. So many people are stuck in their questions and concerns: *When is this breakthrough going to happen, Lord?*

Why did that tragedy happen? I don't understand. It's not fair.
And on and on. All of these thoughts are natural, but they
will weigh you down. They have been given to try to distract you because the last thing the enemy wants is for you
to lift up your head and receive God's joy. When you are
distracted with such heavy burdens, everything else seems
harder. Your soul is crowded. It can get to be too much.

But God is looking for us to recognize the shackles and
redirect our minds. He has come to set us free. He gives us
powerful tools to break out and overcome adversity—to say,
"It is well," no matter what is going on in our circumstances.
He wants us to rejoice in the Lord always, to be anxious for
nothing, to let our requests be made known to God with
thanksgiving in our hearts, and to receive the peace that
passes all understanding. We really can sing praises in the
middle of a crisis and know that God will overcome.

As our family watched the storms go by and sang praises
in the midst of them, we weren't focused on the dark clouds
or heavy rains. We were focused on how the heavens display the glory of God. The storm became a platform for us
to glorify Him and for Him to demonstrate His wonders.
That is a magnificent parable for our lives.

In whatever adversity you face, begin to think about
God's goodness as you come before Him. Like David in
Psalm 103, tell your soul to bless the Lord and forget none
of His benefits. Enter His gates with thanksgiving in your
heart, and as you worship Him, begin to see your breakthrough on the horizon. Your praises move God, and He
will move on your behalf.

Chapter 10

RECOGNIZING DIVINE INVITATION

I HEARD A STORY YEARS AGO that a congregation of about two thousand people received a prophetic word about God's glory being revealed through them to the world. The person prophesying issued an invitation: "If you will stand to receive this word, God will take you to all the nations of the earth to declare His glory." Ruth Heflin and her brother enthusiastically stood up to receive this word for themselves, but when they looked around at the rest of the congregation, they realized they were the only two standing.

Ruth was astonished that an invitation from God Himself was accepted by only two out of two thousand people. "Lord, why isn't everybody standing?" she asked.

"They are all bound by false humility," He answered.

Ruth and her brother did go to many nations to release God's glory; she became a well-known revivalist and had far-reaching impact on many people around the world until her death in 2000. She accepted God's invitation not because she lacked humility but because she knew how God wants to show Himself strong through His people.

I believe the Spirit of God is awakening us in this hour to begin taking off the blinders that limit our thinking. He wants us to be so full of Him that He can't be contained. That has nothing to do with being full of ourselves; it's all about Him. He tells us we are the light of the world. But what good is a light if it's hidden under a basket? Lights are meant to be set on display—on a hilltop or a lamppost, out in the open so people can benefit. Yet many Christians seem to have adopted a false humility that says it's more humble to keep a low profile. That kind of thinking never allows you to dream big or step into your destiny. Real humility allows you to think big thoughts and have big visions and dreams because you know they aren't about you. They are all about God.

In this season, faith is being released in greater measure than ever before. A lot of believers can quote Bible verses that say all things are possible for those who believe and that emphasize God's power to accomplish anything. But these aren't just theological statements; they are invitations. And they are becoming more and more real for people who are willing to take the shackles off their thinking and realize that God wants to do exceedingly abundantly beyond all we can ask or think, as His Word declares.

God wants to give us new eyes. His longing is for us to step fully into the fellowship made possible by the death and resurrection of Jesus. He paid the penalty of sin for us not so we could just talk about being saved but so we could enter into full freedom and an intimate relationship with Him. His heart for each one of us is that we would know the joy of His company and see the delight in His eyes. It's tragic how many believers don't know how much affection God has for them. But that is changing as many are awakening to His freedom and grace and are beginning to see with new eyes. God promises us the mind of Christ, which means we can see as He sees and fully know the hope of our calling. His dreams for us are truly amazing.

THE TEST OF FALSE HUMILITY

One of the greatest tests we will face in the wilderness is the false humility that limits our thinking and keeps us from experiencing all God wants us to experience. The Bible very clearly tells us that all things are possible for those who believe and that God wants to do exceedingly abundantly beyond all we can ask or think. Nowhere does it say, "Who are you to think such big thoughts about yourself? How dare you dream like that!" The Bible never tells us to limit our expectations or tone down our hope. It never equates humility with a hidden, unassuming lifestyle. No, it tells us God does great things, and it invites us to become partners with Him in releasing His glory on earth.

So where do those false, limiting beliefs come from? One place is our culture, which loves to put people in their place and quench fires. People have a competitive nature, and they often put others down in order to feel good about themselves. Big dreams may feel like a threat to those around you, even though there are plenty of dreams to go around. Then sometimes we look at our circumstances and put ourselves down because of them. They may come from a terrible self-image or an inability to see beyond a current situation. Or perhaps we have been taught to protect ourselves from disappointment. Whatever the reason, we find ourselves bound by barriers and shortsightedness, all the while thinking we're just being "realistic." But that isn't realistic at all! Realism is what God says about us, and many people are only beginning to understand what that really means.

When God was first calling me to ministry, I didn't know many prominent women in that role. I knew of Kathryn Kuhlman and Joyce Meyer, but that was about it. Yet I was having big dreams of fireballs going out over crowds and people getting healed. I could envision deep, powerful experiences with God. I once shared these dreams with someone, and the response was very deflating. "I've never really seen that about you," this person said. And my heart fell. But we have to know that these kinds of tests will come from people both inside and outside the church. We have to choose whether to base our hope, trust, and belief on the circumstances around us or on what God says. Will we dare to believe Him, even when those around us don't?

Today God is doing what He showed me when He first called me. The dead are being raised, the deaf are hearing, the sick and dying are being healed, and the fireballs are going out over crowds as people are being healed in their seats. I have the privilege of ministering hope and life to people all over the world. God has truly been faithful.

Will you dare to dream?

It's interesting how God works. I believe the Spirit drops invitations into our minds in the form of thoughts and waits to see who is going to bite. Some people will not recognize those thoughts as invitations. "If only that could have been for me," they think, or, "I wish that could happen, but I can't imagine ever being in that situation." They close up the soil of their heart and won't allow these seeds to be planted in it. But God wants to plant, cultivate, and harvest. We have to let these seeds germinate and take root.

I know people who have daydreams about paralytics walking, cancer disappearing, ears and eyes opening up, and many other major miracles happening. These are wonderful dreams. But some people will have these thoughts and then not be diligent about guarding them. Those dreams become like the seeds in Jesus's parable of the sower that were snatched away by the birds of the air. We have to be deliberate in cooperating with God, first to receive the seeds being planted and then to allow them to germinate in our hearts. We need to receive them with the faith that God wants to release—to see "all things are possible for those who believe" (Mark 9:23) as an invitation.

Do you really believe all things are possible for you? Will you dare to dream? It's not about you becoming big so everyone notices how great you are. It's about Jesus being your life and expressing His life through you. When you wake up to that reality, you realize He must be lifted up in order to draw all people to Himself. That's why the Bible doesn't just say to humble yourself. It says to humble yourself in the sight of the Lord, and He will lift you up (James 4:10; 1 Pet. 5:6). God can trust those with humble hearts enough to lift them up into places of great influence.

People who warn against pride are right in saying that God opposes the proud. But their solution—to stay low and dream small dreams, if you dream any dreams at all— is contrary to God's Word to us. Humility that prevents you from having influence is not a kingdom attitude. If you recognize that everything is all about Jesus, you will be humble and aware with a holy fear of your awesome responsibility to steward Him within you. You'll be as low as you need to be. In fact, the more He does through you, the more you'll realize your need to depend on Him. You'll tremble with hunger and delight. You'll know when someone gets healed that Jesus is the one who did it.

The more you recognize the miracles of God, the more you are brought into an attitude of thanksgiving. And the more you give thanks, the more you will recognize the miraculous power of God at work in your heart. You'll realize that God is the one drawing worship out of your heart, stirring up faith, giving you words to say, and stepping into each situation with His power. It's not only all *about* Him; it's all *from* Him.

I long for the church to come into a new season when we will no longer fuss amongst ourselves and try to pull one another down, and I believe that's beginning to happen. At our church we just celebrate what God is doing. It would be a foreign concept not to be excited for one another and what the Spirit is doing through each of us. And many churches are living in this kind of environment. But sometimes I go places where I sense that people are jealous and trying to prove themselves. It's a snare, and it traps people in very limiting attitudes. Snares are to be broken in this season; it's time to get up and run, to dream with God, to believe, to say all things are possible, and to celebrate whatever He does in other members of the body. Celebrating other people's breakthroughs releases faith for your own.

EMBRACING THE INVITATIONS

The disciples were on a boat on the Sea of Galilee when a storm suddenly whipped up. Jesus, who had gone away to pray for a while, saw the boat being tossed by the wind and waves, and came to it walking on the water. The disciples were terrified, thinking they were seeing a ghost. Who else would be standing on storm-tossed water in the middle of the night? But Jesus, recognizing their fear, identified Himself and told them not to be afraid. So Peter boldly asked for verification. "Lord, if it's you...tell me to come to you on the water" (Matt. 14:28). Jesus did, and Peter got out and walked on the water too.

> *The more you recognize the miracles of God, the more you are brought into an attitude of thanksgiving.*

That's pretty amazing. Peter saw what Jesus was doing and asked to do it too. Jesus didn't issue an elaborate invitation. Jesus didn't even bring up the idea in the first place. Peter saw what was possible and wanted to participate, and he was able to step into something the other disciples didn't even recognize as an opportunity.

That is often what divine invitations look like. God usually doesn't lay the path out in front of us and send us an embossed invitation asking us to begin walking on it. We aren't likely to hear His voice saying, "Please come, let Me use you to perform a miracle for this person." God dresses His invitations up in ways that will require you to see with the eyes of the Spirit, to think with the mind of Christ, and to take steps of faith where no visible path has been prepared. You'll have to see what Jesus is doing and recognize it as a divine invitation. Peter was the only disciple who did that in the middle of the storm, so he was the only one who responded and was able to experience the miracle.

The Spirit is taking us in these days beyond cloudy, hazy dreams and into more literal visions. God still speaks in mysteries and parables, and He always will while we are on this earth. But He also speaks very literally and specifically at times, especially when we don't have time to process His parables and need clarity on a situation. This is a season of acceleration, and He isn't waiting on us to spend a bit more time climbing religious ladders in order to qualify for His great works. He doesn't want us sitting around waiting for an invitation. He wants us to recognize the invitations that are there and are already quite clear.

Many of today's prophetic voices are united in identifying this time as a season of open doors. It's as if God has set up a huge banqueting table and is waiting for us to decide what to do with it. Will we wait for an invitation?

Wonder if it's really for us? Pick and choose a little bit here and there as though we're unwelcome guests? Or will we come and eat with an enormous appetite?

God's desire is for us to open our hearts and let the King of Glory come in. He's waiting to arise and shine through us. But we have to be able to recognize the invitations. I've been praying from the Book of Revelation lately that God would give me eye salve so I can see things as they truly are (Rev. 3:18), and He has been answering that in really glorious ways. I believe if we ask Him to, He will open our eyes to the invitations that are everywhere around us—far more than we have ever recognized. Those little daydreams, those new ideas, those visions of people getting healed and God being glorified—these are not distractions to swat away like flies. They are the Spirit trying to drop a thought in our hearts. He wants us to be like Mary and say, "Let it be to me according to your word" (Luke 1:38, NKJV). Allow those thoughts to be implanted in your spirit. Say, "Yes, Lord, I'll receive that and believe it. Thank You." Begin to believe and declare it. When you start to come into agreement with your own mouth, the seeds of those God-inspired dreams will begin to take root.

The first time I walked into an Anglican cathedral in the UK, I felt so burdened for the people. I could feel the heart of God burning for them. I turned to my friend and said, "I'm going to preach in the Anglican cathedrals of England." I held on to that thought and cultivated it. Six months later, I had invitations to preach in several Anglican cathedrals. All it took was seeing the thought as an invitation and coming into agreement with it.

You have to be careful who is around you when you speak things like this; you don't want to cast your pearls before those who will trample on them rather than appreciate them. I have a lot of people around me who know how this works. I'll make some wild statement, and they realize what's happening. "You're playing the game aren't you? OK, I'll agree with that. And I'm coming with you when it happens." They understand because they've seen it work out. You need people who "get it." Not everyone will. But begin to declare things as God's invitation, and watch how He opens doors.

You may feel that you are in the midst of some very limiting circumstances. You may have ideas that you think are from God but wonder how in the world He will ever accomplish them. But if you'll receive what the Spirit is implanting in you, you will receive faith to rise up and say, "All things are possible. God will make a way where there seems to be no way. My God is for me, so who can be against me? When He opens a door, who can shut it?" If God is the one who has purposed something, He will find ways to accomplish it. He will bring it about if you cooperate with Him in faith. He is faithful to do what He says He will do.

This is not hard work. It's a joy. The assignments God is handing out are good ones. You want them. You have only one life to live for Him, so live it well. Begin to lay hold of the things He has for you. If there are assignments others won't take because of false humility or listening to discouraging lies, step in and take them yourself. Get all God has for you. He wants to take your life and make it a bright, shining light for His glory. We must lay hold of what God has for us and steward it well.

DREAMS AND DISCIPLINE

I've always been pretty good at "winging it." In grade school I entered a talent competition without really having a plan. I sang an Evie Tornquist song for the music section and came up with some gymnastic moves for the miscellaneous section. As there were only two entrants in the miscellaneous section, the school decided to send a note home to my mother saying they needed another entrant at the grand finale. But they added, "Could your daughter actually prepare something this time?"

When I got to twelfth grade and had to fill out the form that declares what kind of university courses I might apply for, I used the same approach. I decided I wanted to be a music teacher. The problem was that you had to have an instrument for auditions. I was a singer, and I hadn't had any lessons, so I needed an instrument. So at the last minute I decided to take up piano.

For someone used to winging it, I did pretty well. I focused on a standard piano piece for a few weeks and learned it well enough to pass the audition to get in as a piano major. It was a miracle; although my grades were good, I was new at the piano. Yet I had decided that was what I was going to do, and by the grace of God I got in.

I began my studies as a music major, fully unaware that nearly everyone else there had been playing their instrument since they were six years old. And when it was time for my first exam, I was asked to play a scale. I didn't know how to play more than two octaves, which was about a third grade level and not nearly enough for university standards. To my shock and horror, I failed my exam. I was stunned. I failed? I could hardly believe it. I wasn't used to failing. I had always gotten by, even when I had to wing it.

For the rest of my three-year degree, I had to spend three hours every single day, including holidays and weekends, practicing the piano. I had to develop discipline like I had never known it before. It's not like I had never worked for anything in my life; I certainly had. But I had never had to work at this level of daily discipline. I didn't even know what that kind of discipline looked like. I couldn't afford to miss time. When I went to visit my father on holidays, I would go to the local school and ask if I could do my three hours of practice on their piano because my father didn't have one. For a girl who always liked to wing it, this was a very new experience. I began to understand the importance and value of discipline.

Discipline is not a very popular word in some Christian circles, is it? It can have negative connotations, perhaps because we associate it with legalism, dead works, or raw willpower—efforts that may not be empowered by the Spirit or flow with the way the Spirit is moving. We love freedom, and discipline can seem so contrary to it. And it's true that discipline can become a matter of self-effort that is divorced from God, and we don't want any part of that. We don't want dead works. We want to do as we feel. We want to "wing it" through life.

I can understand that. I love the flow of the Spirit. I want only to move where God moves and say what He says. I want to be so under His influence that I point in whichever direction His wind is blowing. But to do that, I actually need to be disciplined and undistracted. I need to have doves' eyes as described in the Song of Songs. Did you know doves have no peripheral vision? They can see only what they focus on. Without allowing the Lord to train us to live disciplined lives, we can waste so much precious time that He intended us to use being fruitful. If we don't practice discipline, we risk entering the promise without knowing how to actually live in it. Our modern world has endless distractions vying for our attention. God has given us power to have doves' eyes, and it is in the wilderness that we discover just how important it is to maintain a disciplined focus. We begin to cry out, like David, for the "one thing" (Ps. 27:4).

God wants us, like the sons of Issachar, to be aware of the times and seasons so we can maximize the opportunities each season brings. We must be fully aware and fully awake to take advantage of every opportunity and every invitation He is giving. The ability to wing it is a wonderful gift, but discipline brings greater rewards.

I'm very aware of this on days when I have back-to-back meetings. I have a standing, scheduled meeting on my calendar where I can have some quality time with God. I try to have that time every morning, as well as our family devotions, a little more with Him in the afternoon, and in the evening again before I go to sleep. When it comes to God, I definitely like three meals a day and snacks! Of course, I like to practice being aware of the fellowship of the Holy Spirit throughout all my activities, knowing that He is my ever-present help and longs for me to lean on Him to help me with everything. But in order to keep the one thing David wrote about as my priority, I need quality devotion time with the Lord every day. I can't afford to wing it. On the days when I do, I really just coast on the gifts and miss out on the full experience of power that only comes from waiting on Him. "Those who wait on the LORD shall renew their strength. They shall mount up with wings like eagles, they shall run and not be weary, they shall walk and not faint" (Isa. 40:31, NKJV).

I wake up in the morning praying. I ask God what He was saying in my dreams; He speaks so regularly in them that I take time to listen. I make decrees, and I talk to God about the things that are on my heart. The time I spend with God is even more necessary than meeting with the ministry team when we're preparing for a conference or dealing with the day-to-day demands of family and ministry. The more I'm doing, the more I actually need to discipline myself to take time to talk to God. And if I don't schedule it, the time seems to get taken up with something else pressing for my attention. My heart says He is my first priority, but discipline helps me make it a reality. Like the saying goes, I'm too busy not to pray!

Wouldn't that be horrible? A pastor trying to get through her day without some time alone in prayer sounds a bit scandalous, doesn't it? Yet that's what so many of us do when we get busy. We let that time get crowded out, and we try to get by without any time of refreshing or processing with God. We "go with the flow," but the flow of life doesn't lead us into prayer time if other demands are squeezing it out. I actually have to take the time to declare this relationship with the Lord to be what is most important in my life. And I do that by prioritizing it on my schedule.

That's why discipline is such a necessary part of dreaming. Dreams very often don't come to pass unless we live in the discipline necessary for them. We have to take the time to prioritize so our priorities—the dreams God has put within us—can really take first place in our lives. Otherwise, they get squeezed out and are left unfulfilled.

I believe we are being offered an invitation like no other generation has ever been offered. We have stepped into a new era—I feel it so strongly—in which we need to be fully aware. We need to wake up and recognize what's going on. This is the year of the favor of the Lord. It's time to begin to dream like we never have before.

THE URGENCY OF THE HOUR

Let me paint a picture of this season for you. God is moving. He is calling His people into a deeper relationship with Him and waking people up to the truth of who He really is. We are seeing miracles we used to only dream about. Diseases are being healed, addictions are being broken, and people are being saved. People all over the world are being provoked to worship God with fresh awe as they see His power at work. We are entering a greater harvest of souls than we have ever seen, and it's a glorious time to be alive. God has put so many good works in front of us that exceed our wildest dreams. He wants to use us in demonstrations of His power.

Meanwhile, many believers are wasting a lot of time on Facebook or YouTube, or consuming entertainment that really does nothing for us other than eat up our schedule. These things aren't bad in themselves, but it's amazing how much time slips away when we aren't being intentional about how we use it. Do we really want to go through these exciting times distracted by things that don't last and don't ultimately matter?

I believe the Holy Spirit is giving revelation of the urgency of this hour, and only the disciplined and repentant will fully participate in what He is doing. If you choose to steward your time, your gifts, and your resources wisely, you will be given more. That's how God's kingdom works. Those who are faithful with what they have will receive more. And in this season of harvest and miracles, I have to believe most of us want more.

It is interesting that God's invitations don't always come in fancy envelopes in the mail. They are often subtle nudges, ideas that He drops into our spirit. The Bible tells us that He gives us the desires of our heart as we delight ourselves in Him (Ps. 37:4). That means when we live with a heavenly mind-set, aware that we have the mind of Christ, very often the desires that spring up in our hearts are divine invitations that await our response. He puts the desires in our heart! Like Mary, when we recognize these divine invitations to partner with God's purposes, we need to say, "Let it be to me according to your word" (Luke 1:38, NKJV).

God created us to think like He does, and His ideas are glorious. And we get to be a part of what He is doing! He is so good to draw us into His plans and let us partner with Him to restore lives and grow His kingdom.

But it's one thing to say, "Yes, Lord, this is good," and another to actually discipline ourselves to say, "Lord, how do You want me to steward what You're dropping into my spirit?" He gives us the dream, but He actually wants us to walk around on the inside of it—to really see it with the eyes of our sanctified imagination and to cooperate with Him as He shows us the detail. He wants to take us into the height, the depth, the width, and the breadth of what He is saying. But seeing the dream is just the beginning. We then have to discipline ourselves to deliberately cooperate with what He is doing and begin to be alert to steward it.

The wonderful thing is that as we steward what God has given us, He will give more. That's great news for those of us who long for more. This is a really easy way to get it. All we have to do is recognize God's invitations, grab them, and do something with them. If we steward His invitations well, He will offer us more.

If you look at discipline from that perspective, it no longer looks like hard work or self-effort, does it? It's very simple. When you begin to recognize God's voice and His dreams, it is easy to get excited and marvel over what you perceived. But stewarding it well means taking initiative and doing something. One of the best ways to start is by making declarations about what God is going to do. There is creative, prophetic power in your words. You were created in the image of God, who created the world with His words. Life and death are in the power of the tongue. When I recognize the Lord giving me a desire from His heart, I come into agreement with it, declaring that thing as His will, and I speak about it as though it was already happening. When you start to get an inkling of something God is doing, align yourself with it. Speak it out. Declare it as though it's already happening, knowing that God wants to bring it to pass.

Our ministry team does this regularly, and it has become our favorite game. It started during a time when I was feeling very discouraged over a situation with one of my children. Often when I was travelling and doing back-to-back meetings, people would inevitably ask me over breakfast how things were going with that situation. I began to dread the question, as just thinking about it would send me spiraling toward depression. So I began taking charge of the conversation before it could go there. Every morning over breakfast, I would ask my friends if they would like to play a game. I'd explain that they could say something that was in their heart as though it was already happening. I'd make declarations like, "People get out of wheelchairs in my meetings. Creative miracles are regular occurrences in my meetings. I am healthy and happy, and all my children love God and are married to godly spouses." (Despite the fact that none of them were yet of the age to be married, this was a happy thought, and I knew it was God's will.) This game would continue as we'd go around and around the circle, and you could feel the atmosphere become charged with faith and hope. And pretty soon my declarations started coming to pass in astounding ways.

> *Speak it out. Declare it as though*
> *it's already happening, knowing that*
> *God wants to bring it to pass.*

Whenever I am with my interns, we still play my game, speaking out and declaring things that are not as though they are. They have become good dreamers, and many are now doing great exploits for God! When you're walking in fellowship with God and the Holy Spirit puts something in your heart and shows you how He wants to accomplish it through your life, that's an invitation for you to shine with His glory. Though some may feel nervous about being so bold, you don't have to come up with things you want Him to do in your life on your own inspiration. He puts a dream, sometimes even just the first part of a dream, into your heart, and that dream will make Him glorious. Why would anyone shrink back from that?

The Father is extending an invitation to come into agreement with what He wants to do. Declare what He is saying, and then watch it come to be.

Chapter 11

WAGING WAR WITH THE PROMISES

*I*T WAS NINE days before my thirty-first birthday, and it had been a horrible year. I had endured some terrible situations that had left me feeling unjustly treated, misunderstood, and discouraged. And the dream I had held in my heart since I was twenty-three felt impossible. The Lord had promised me that He was going to open doors to public ministry when I was thirty. And I was going to be thirty for only a few more days.

When I was a young woman, the Lord magnificently delivered me from so much and showed me His face as He set me free. Very soon after, I started having visions of myself calling out to the lost to be saved—those visions I mentioned earlier of fireballs going out over crowds as I preached and people being miraculously healed. I would see people getting up out of wheelchairs as the presence of God set them free. And although it all seemed so unlikely to me, God confirmed His call to me in a variety of ways. He spoke to me through the lives of Joseph and Jesus, how they had been brought into public ministry at the age of thirty. And I felt the Lord say He wanted to do the same for me. So I did what I knew to do. I went to Bible college to prepare. But seven years later, I still had not seen God open any doors, and my life seemed to be falling apart around me.

So that morning just a few days before my birthday, as I

was lamenting my plight to God, I got militant in my desperation. I began to remind God of His promise. I heard myself saying to God, "You said the doors would open in my thirtieth year. Well, here I am, and there are only a few more days until I turn thirty-one. I know You are faithful to do what You promised!" I fixed my gaze on God, waiting for Him to make the next move. I thought that maybe if I had understood how to put action to my faith earlier instead of wallowing in depression for months, things might have happened already. I knew the past could not be changed, but I also knew God had a plan for the future, so I asked Him, "Lord, what now? What do You want me to do?" Then the Lord spoke, "Why don't you get up and go to that conference I've been putting on your heart?"

So I did. I got up, went to the conference, sat down, and ended up next to a woman named Faylene Sparkes, who was one of the most recognized prophets in Australia at the time. The Lord spoke to her while we were sitting in the congregation, and she turned to me and invited me to have lunch with her. As we talked over lunch, she said she felt the Holy Spirit was telling her to invite me to begin traveling with her. It was highly unusual, to say the least, but effortless and clearly orchestrated by God. Just like that the doors God had promised to open began to open. Since that time, I have seen so many people saved, healed, delivered, and baptized in the Holy Spirit, and I've seen God do more amazing miracles than I can record. I have planted churches and am now preaching the gospel all around the world. God truly is faithful to do what He promised. I just needed to learn how to "wage war" with His promise. (See 1 Timothy 1:18.)

WHEN THINGS LOOK HOPELESS

In the Book of Judges we read about a time when Israel had been subject to their enemy the Midianites for several years, and were feeling very powerless and discouraged. Every time Israel sowed seeds and cultivated their fields, the Midianites would come to steal and destroy the harvest. Like locusts they devoured everything Israel produced. God's people remained stuck in poverty and lack, and all they knew to do was to cry out to God for help.

That's how it was in the days before God raised up Gideon as a leader (Judg. 6). That's also how it is for many believers today, especially if they are coming up out of a wilderness. When you're just on the brink of seeing a harvest, the fight gets really intense. The fires of adversity get much hotter, and opposition becomes even more intimidating. The enemy can't ultimately stop your harvest, but he can distract you from it or delay it. He can intimidate you and make you want to run away. He can eat up what God has sown in your heart. But God has plans for you to walk in miracles, and He is asking you to trust Him. He wants to show Himself strong and be glorified in the midst of what looks like impossible circumstances. He is waiting to be your helper.

Like the Israelites, begin to cry out to God. You can't manage things on your own; we aren't designed that way. Acknowledge Him and ask Him for help. Get completely honest and bring everything before Him—every worry, every discouraging thought, every fear. The Holy Spirit will help you in all your troubles, but He is waiting to be asked. He is waiting to cover and help you, and longs for continuous, ongoing, engaging fellowship with you. He wants to be your best friend, not only in theory but in practice. As you present your needs and concerns to Him in faith, His perfect love begins to cast out fear. Faith begins to rise up and expect the answer to every need. You will know you aren't walking alone.

That's what Israel did, and God came and spoke to a man named Gideon. Gideon was hiding in fear, but God began to speak to his identity, calling him a mighty warrior despite every appearance to the contrary. As Gideon stepped into his true self, God led him in a plan to set Israel free from the oppression of Midian and its allies. That's how it always is with God. We cry out; He has a plan. So God raised up Gideon, who began to amass an army.

> *God wants to show Himself strong and be glorified in the midst of what looks like impossible circumstances.*

Gideon managed to pull together about thirty-two thousand men, but that paled in comparison to the size of the armies coming against them. The alliance was huge, but Israel could at least rejoice that someone was finally doing something. But God came to Gideon with a surprising command. Israel's army, already greatly outnumbered by the enemy, was apparently "too many" from God's perspective. He didn't want anyone in Israel to give credit to the army. He wanted it to be absolutely clear that He was the one who delivered them. So He told Gideon to send home everyone who was afraid, and twenty-two thousand left while only ten thousand remained (Judg. 7:3).

This is not unusual when you're about to see a breakthrough. Just when you think the time of victory is coming, things often get worse. You lose resources or energy or motivation. You are put in a place that's even more impossible than before. And it may look like you've lost your opportunity.

When God spoke to me at the age of twenty-three about

releasing me into ministry when I was thirty, I did what I knew to prepare for it. I went to Bible college. I set my heart on the time of release. And in my thirtieth year, even just a few days before my thirty-first birthday, things looked worse than ever. The promise appeared impossible. But that is when God brought breakthrough—at the most hopeless point. I've seen this happen so often since then that now I almost laugh. When things start to go wrong, I get excited. I know something wonderful is about to happen. It's another opportunity for God to demonstrate how glorious He is.

YOU HAVE A CHOICE

God gave Gideon's army a choice. Anyone who was afraid could leave. God gives us that freedom too; we don't have to step into anything we don't want to step into. We can leave our destiny waiting. When we became believers in Jesus, God gave us the power to be different from the way we were. Things on the inside began to change. But our calling and our victory didn't become inevitable. We have to choose them. And the enemy will come along and tell us it's not worth it, or he'll distract us from the joy and abundance that are set apart for us. And God will let us fall prey to those distractions if we so choose.

God's plans for you are brilliant. If you saw them fully, you would agree. He wants to lead you into a life more abundant, an experience that is above all you can ask or think, more glorious than you've imagined. But the way to enter in is not just to acknowledge how you feel and nurse those feelings. It isn't to give in to whatever the flesh is dictating or to the distractions that are pulling you away— or to the temptation of dropping out and not pressing forward. You don't have to press forward if you don't want to; God gives you that choice. But it's not a good choice.

That is why God tells you to lean not on your own understanding but acknowledge Him in all your ways (Prov. 3:5–6). That is when He makes your paths straight.

Think through what that promise means. When you've been praying and crying out for God to help you in whatever problem you're facing—your family situation, your career or finances, your ministry—He's asking you to begin to acknowledge Him in all your ways. Instead of being led by how you feel, you can begin to declare His promises and release your burdens to Him. But if you then get up and continue to worry about it, you're missing out on whatever God has set up for you to walk into. If you've asked Him for help, let it go. Actually trust that He's going to help, and be willing to walk in the way He directs. We can only receive what God gives and take back what the enemy has stolen by leaning on God, acknowledging Him, asking Him what He wants to do and how He wants to do it, and then moving forward with Him.

The promise of Proverbs 3:5–6 is backed up by another one in Psalm 32:8–9: "I will instruct you and teach you in the way you should go; I will counsel you with my loving eye on you. Do not be like the horse or the mule, which have no understanding but must be controlled by bit and bridle or they will not come to you." He wants to direct, but not without your awareness. He wants you to be an active participant in the solution.

God is delighted to lead you. He loves when you cry out to Him for help. He wants you to get up from your prayer and look at His face. Where is He looking? Where is He going? What is He doing? Acknowledge Him and His ways. The Hebrew word for "acknowledge" means "to be intimate with." So if you have been praying for breakthrough in your work, for example, there's more to the answer than getting up, going to work, and thinking, "I hope He does something. We'll see what happens." No, you go in alert, thinking, "Lord, I'm here. Show me what You want me to say. Show me opportunities. What are we going to do today? Show me what You want me to see. Help me be fully aware and fully awake to Your work."

When you spend time talking to the Holy Spirit, it delights His heart. But His answer is more than "OK, I'll help." It's "Yes! Come on! Let's go! Look at My face. I'll guide you with My eye. I'll lead you into the breakthrough. I'll show you the divine appointments you've been looking for. I'll take you there." The power of prayer is not so much in the prayer itself as it is in the fellowship with God that comes afterward. When you pray for help, turn your full attention to the Lord.

> *God is delighted to lead you. He loves when you cry out to Him for help.*

When you make your choice to stay with the army that's moving forward, resolve not to go back. The enemy will come in and tell you everything you're missing—the party scene, affirmation from the popular people, the leisure time you're missing out on, the "freedoms" you're giving up. And it's true; you have the option to do those things if you want. But you don't have the option of both staying behind and going forward. It's one or the other. The question is, what does your spirit really want? Is it really in your heart to give in to fear, distraction, apathy, convenience, or anything else? Or is it really in your heart to go forward, overcome, recover all, and step into your destiny? Those who know their God—who are intimately acquainted with Him—will be strong and do great exploits. You are free to choose whatever you'd like, but deep in your heart, you want spiritual fruitfulness rather than spiritual slumber. God puts life and death before you and urges you to choose life.

Keeping Your Focus

Gideon's army was left with ten thousand men after twenty-two thousand went home. From all outward appearances, it was much less equipped to deal with the enemy than before. But God said ten thousand was still too many. Gideon had to be scratching his head at this point. How could God not be glorified by a victory with only ten thousand men? But that's what God said, and He instructed Gideon to take the army to the water and separate them into two groups. Those who cupped water into their hands and then lapped it up with their tongues were put in one group. Those who knelt down and put their faces to the water were in the other group. Most of the men got on their knees to drink, but three hundred cupped the water in their hands. Gideon was surely hoping the larger group would remain, but that isn't how God works. He chose to save Israel through the three hundred, and He had Gideon send the rest home (Judg. 7:4–8).

> *You don't have the option of both staying behind and going forward. It's one or the other.*

What was the point of this division at the watering hole? I believe it's a picture of believers and the battles we face. God does nothing by accident; this situation was a shadow of a very important truth we need to understand today. Those soldiers who were just focused on getting their needs met, regardless of the situation around them, were sent home. Those who remained alert, aware of what was going on around them rather than focused exclusively on their needs, were kept. They were certainly in the minority, but they were enough for God to win the victory. He can accomplish far more through a small group of dedicated, alert believers than He can through a large group of self-focused believers.

I love it when I see people who are going through a hard time looking to love and minister to someone else. They are very aware of their own wilderness, but they know God still wants to shine through them during that difficult situation and meet the needs of others. They are in pain, but they care more about the pain of those around them. Instead of obsessing about the prayers that haven't been answered yet, they are letting God work through them to answer the longings of other people. It's a vital attitude to have in the wilderness. God looks at that and says, "I can do great things through this one."

God is searching for this kind of army. He can do a lot through people who pursue their calling no matter what else they are going through. You might be going through a hard time, but if your hard time is preventing you from reaching out to somebody else, the enemy sees that as an effective weapon against you. He will keep you in your wilderness as long as he can because it is working to immobilize you. But if you know you are a minister of reconciliation, a light in this world, a gift of God to the earth, you will live in that calling even before you have any kind of breakthrough. Like Gideon's men who were prepared for battle before a battle existed, you will be prepared for breakthrough before breakthrough happens. And God delights in choosing you for the victory.

If you are experiencing a time of deeper-than-usual need, resist the temptation to become obsessed with receiving a blessing and take every opportunity to be a blessing to God and others. You can still get your needs met; God wants to take care of you. But He doesn't want your focus to turn inward. Focus instead on manifesting Jesus to someone else. If Jesus is living in you, there is no wilderness that can prevent you from offering a word of knowledge, an expression of hope, or an act of love to others. When you do those kinds of things, the river begins to flow. You receive far more when you're giving than you do when you're focused on receiving. What you give will come back to you in abundance.

It is vitally important to be deliberate in this, recognizing that Christ in you is the hope of glory. As with the servants who were stewarding the master's talents, God is not looking for you to take what He has given and bury it in the ground (Matt. 25:14–30). He is looking for you to steward what you have, even in the dry seasons of life. You don't have to wait for someone to prophesy and give you permission; you already have His commission to be as He is in this world.

SEEING THE PROMISE

Now down to three hundred, Gideon's army was ready for whatever God had planned. It's interesting that on the night of battle, God told Gideon that he could sneak down to the enemy camp and eavesdrop if he was afraid and needed encouragement. Gideon chose to eavesdrop, acknowledging that he was in fact afraid. Yet earlier, when God sent all the fearful soldiers home, Gideon didn't volunteer to leave. Perhaps it would have been a bit too awkward for the leader to admit his fear and return home, but the fact that Gideon didn't do that shows that he was not being led by his emotions. How he felt and what his spirit really wanted were two different things. So Gideon stayed, and on the night of battle, he went down to the enemy camp to listen in. He overheard one enemy soldier telling another of a dream, and the other interpreted it as Gideon's victory over Midian. Gideon worshipped God and, emboldened by the dream, went back to his men to prepare for battle.

Gideon already had a promise from God as well as God's instructions. What more did he need? Apparently, he also needed a picture. He needed to see the promise. God could have demanded that Gideon act solely on the promise he already received. That should have been enough. But He understands our hearts and is kind to give us what we need. So while He waits for us to respond to His promise, He doesn't wait without also giving us everything we need to hold on in faith. He gives us a picture of what He is promising.

This gift God has given us is called an imagination. Many people think that using your imagination to visualize things is evil or a tool of New Age spirituality. That's because imagination can be misused just as easily as it can be used. But God gave us our imagination as a powerful, precious gift, and He wants us to use it to see His promises. He did that with Abraham, telling him to look at the stars in the sky and the sand on the shore as examples of how numerous his descendants would be (Gen. 22:17). Until Abraham got the picture, it was a vague promise. Afterward, he could conceive it. Jesus did the same in commissioning Peter, telling him to launch out into the deep and cast his net. When he pulled up a boatload of fish, Peter got a visual of what it means to be a fisher of men with an overflowing harvest (Luke 5:1–11). This happens again and again in Scripture, and God will do it with you too. If you will cultivate the vision in your imagination, God will shape it and let you see what the promise looks like.

When God commissions you into ministry, He wants

you to see it, to imagine it, to spend time thinking about what it's going to look like. I've been doing this for years. I would imagine deaf ears opening and cloudy eyes beginning to see. I'd imagine people getting up out of wheelchairs or coming back from the doctor's office with reports of being cancer-free. Those daydreams may seem like wasted time to many people, but they aren't wasted time at all. They are part of the process of getting clear pictures of God's promises and desires. If we've submitted our minds to Him and invited Him to inspire our imaginations, we can trust Him to write on the screens of our minds. Our imagination is sanctified when we submit it to God; it is the canvas on which God can paint His plans for us. If you can see the promises of God there, you can have them. When you get a promise from Him, begin to see it and say it, and He will give it to you.

Gideon got a picture of victory and was provoked to worship. When we can start to celebrate and thank God for the victory before it actually comes, it positions us to receive the promise. That's why God is able to tell the barren to sing and celebrate (Isa. 54:1). He is giving them a picture of the fruitfulness to come.

> *When God commissions you into ministry, He wants you to see it, to imagine it, to spend time thinking about what it's going to look like.*

The enemy will try to use your imagination too. He comes to write fears and doubts on the screen of your mind. He fills your thoughts with pictures of everything that could go wrong and distorts the true picture of God's promise. His lies exalt themselves above the knowledge of Jesus—the faithful one. A key aspect of casting down his lies is putting the truth up in their place. If you are praying for someone to get saved, don't see that person's current condition; see him or her worshipping, ministering, and burning with the radiance of God. If you are believing God for healing, don't envision how to cope with the symptoms or what it will be like when they get worse. Think about what it will feel like when you're healed; envision your restoration, and get happy about it. When you're able to enter into joy before the breakthrough, you're in a great position to receive it.

Albert Einstein said, "Imagination is everything. It is the preview of life's coming attractions."[1] I love that quote. He also said imagination is more important than knowledge, which is quite something for someone who had so much knowledge.[2] Even the carnal world understands the power of imagination. But it isn't a worldly thing at all, at least not in the way the Spirit uses it in your life. He wants to give you a preview of life's coming attractions and for you to focus on them.

POSSESS WHAT YOU PURSUE

I believe we will not possess anything that we are unwilling to pursue. I don't mean that we have to work for everything; God often drops generous gifts into our lives that we didn't have to run after. But when He gives a promise, He doesn't expect us to just sit there and wait for it. We have to be willing to pursue it. It was the same with the promise He gave to Israel—to bring them into a land flowing with milk and honey. They had to go through the wilderness to get there, and those who could not envision God bringing them into it never arrived. Only two from the Exodus generation, Joshua and Caleb, actually inherited the promise, because they were the only ones who could see it with eyes of faith. A promise is meaningless unless you picture it, believe it, *and* pursue it. Even seeing it is not enough if you're not willing to step out as the Spirit leads and pursue what He has promised.

> *"Imagination is everything. It is the preview of life's coming attractions." —Albert Einstein*

I'm not suggesting you move out in your own strength. Hold His hand and listen for His instructions. He is very good to lead and to help wherever we need it. He empowers. But we still have to follow.

Believe me, this is far better than filling your life with rubbish. God gives you the freedom to do as you please, but you were built for glory. Your spirit has come alive, and you are called to walk in greater works than you've even imagined. You were designed for fruitfulness, and you are ready to begin grabbing hold of it and saying yes to God. Acknowledge the promises He has given, picture them and declare them, move with Him to position yourself for them, and celebrate them even now.

I really believe the Holy Spirit is going to bring to pass those things that have been brewing on the inside. Now is the time when you will begin to see breakthrough like never before. We are standing on the cusp of an accelerated season that will take us beyond what we've ever seen before. But we have to remember that there is no victory without a battle. The battle belongs to Him, and we get to fight a fight He has already won. But we still have to persevere and hang on to our confidence in Him.

PRAYING THE WORD

Changes are coming, but only for those who will respond to what God is saying, grab hold of His promises, and pursue them with focus and persistence. He is looking for those who will push through fear, discouragement, and doubt, fixing their hope on Him. Jesus longs for a bride who actually lives for Him rather than one that turns back and lives for herself.

So what has God promised you? What can you see? What has He planted in your heart? You may be able to think of several things immediately, but even if you've never had a prophetic word or clear vision, the Word of God says you can lay hands on the sick and they shall recover. So that's a great place to start if you're looking for a promise to grab hold of. And there are even more in Scripture to receive. Pray some of the prayers in the Word. I've recently been praying the prayer of Jabez for myself, for my church, and for my family. (See 1 Chronicles 4:9–10.) I know from that prayer (and many others) that it's the will of God to bless me. He wants to enlarge my territory and give me more influence. I realized after declaring the prayer of Jabez for a while that the blessings began to multiply. I was receiving more invitations to minister in various places, more churches were being established, and more miracles were happening

But don't stop with the explicit promises in Scripture. Ask for more vision that pertains to you personally. Pray for God to give you a clear picture of what He's calling you to do. Surrender your imagination to His Spirit and begin imagining what it will look like. He has laid up good works in advance for you to do, and He's waiting for you to take His hand and acknowledge Him in everything. Like Israel, cry out to God and ask for His help every step of the way. Like Gideon, push through fear and trust God's power, no matter how weak or strong you feel, even if things seem to get worse before they get better. Eventually promises are fulfilled because God is entirely faithful.

My spirit has been trembling with a glorious shaking. Just as Jesus woke up Lazarus—a name that literally means "God is help"—He is waking up His people now in order to help. He wants to help with your prayer time in the morning, your work time during the day, your family time whenever you're together, your recreational time, your ministry, and every other area of your life. He wants to bring you into a life more abundant than anything you could experience on your own.

God's ways are so much better than ours. When we lean on our own understanding, we end up frustrated and living far below the glory of God's calling. But what would it look like if you actually believed, deep in your heart at every level, that God had your best interests in mind every moment of every day? I used to be afraid that if I surrendered all of myself to Him, I'd end up praying all the time and never get anything else done. But God loves my family, my church, and the desires of my heart. He knows my needs and my dreams. He will never lead me to a place that ignores anything important to my life and calling. And He can do things far better than I can do them on my own.

Trust Him. Acknowledge Him in everything, even when things start to look worse rather than better. Anticipate the deliverance that is coming. Expect breakthrough. He will lead you into great exploits. He will bring you into a place where you are full of His joy at all times.

Chapter 12

DELIGHTING IN GOD

EARS AGO WHEN I went to church meetings I used to get frustrated with all the happy people. That's because I had an agenda: I really wanted everyone else to get on with the serious business of seeking God. It has been almost two decades since that period when I was offended at the laughter, but I remember it well. The problem wasn't so much that people were laughing; I'm all for everyone having a good time. But so much was weighing on me spiritually that I assumed anyone who wasn't burdened and seeking God with a serious face was not altogether spiritual. I was serious about my walk with God, and I thought everyone else should be serious about theirs too.

I've shared how God got me past those assumptions and led me to understand the joy of His presence. Sometimes that joy comes right away, but sometimes you have to keep pressing in for it, seeking Him and training yourself to think and feel the truth about Him. Sometimes you have to tell your soul, "I don't care if you're feeling downcast. Bless the Lord. He is my hope, my answer, my everything. He has promised me fullness of joy in His presence, so that's where we're going. And I'm not letting go until I have it."

Sometimes when we're worshipping God in the wilderness, we begin to taste the breakthrough. A taste is good, but it's not enough, is it? God doesn't promise us just a taste of joy. He promises us fullness (Ps. 16:11). In that place of joy, we don't feel upset or anxious, we aren't tired or burned out, and we aren't sad or depressed. That place of joy is an overflowing sense of delight. That's what we're after. We want to be so full that we overflow.

How many Christians do you know who live in that place of absolute joy? If you look across the church as a whole— not just the believers you spend your time with, but the entire body of Christ—it seems that the majority are not there. I don't mean that in a condemning way; my point is that God has offered us an incredible privilege, and many of us are missing it due to stress, anxiety, fear, discouragement, and the weight of daily burdens and responsibilities. If you look at the faces of Christians and non-Christians, you don't always see a difference in their countenance. But God promises that those who look to Him will be radiant (Ps. 34:5). As we behold Him, we become like Him. As we spend time in His presence, we enter into joy. This is the privilege of every believer, and we don't want to miss out on it.

I've mentioned earlier that a key aspect of getting through the wilderness is stewarding well the things we've been given in the wilderness. Much of that stewardship involves our focus. Our emotional state as believers is determined by what we're focusing on. If we choose to look into the face of the Lord—not just for a pick-me-up during a weekly worship service but all the time—His joy will be available to us. We can fully lay hold of everything that He has laid out for us, and that includes the absolute, unbridled joy and delight of His presence.

DELIGHTING IN GOD ABOVE ALL

A very subtle shift can take place when we seek to delight in God. He has promised us that if we delight ourselves in Him, He will give us the desires of our hearts (Ps. 37:4). That is a wonderful promise, and we can take it quite literally. But what often happens, especially in a wilderness

season, is that we begin to delight in the desires themselves rather than in the God who gives them. We can
get really happy when things start working out, when He
begins to satisfy our desires and we get a taste of that fulfillment. But it's so easy in those times to delight more in
what God is giving than we do in the Giver Himself.

> *Our emotional state as believers is*
> *determined by what we're focusing on.*

Many people, hungry for fulfillment and desperate for
a way out of their wilderness, attend worship services to
encounter God and hear from Him. But they are looking
for a prophetic word about their circumstances more than
they are looking for a relationship with the Father. Their
hearts are more focused on worshipping in order to receive
something than worshipping because He is worthy. Do you
see the difference? One attitude is delight in His gifts; the
other is actually delight in Him. And His promise of satisfying our desires is given only to those who delight in Him.

That is really for our own good. If we delight in the
desires themselves, we will be really happy when things
are working out and really disappointed when they aren't.
That is a very up-and-down way to live, and it isn't ultimately satisfying. There can be a lot of highs in that lifestyle, but there are also a lot of crashes. But if we delight
ourselves in the Lord, we are rooted in someone who does
not change and will not let us down. That's the kind of
hope that does not disappoint.

Truly delighting in God does not mean coming to
Him thinking, "Lord, I'm going to delight in You so I can
receive that promise from You." That may look like worship, but it's really a focus on the desires rather than on
God. He wants instead for us to be able to let it all go—to

delight in Him without even thinking about our desires. He wants us to echo the words of Habakkuk, who resolved that he would praise God whether there was any fruit on the vine or not (Hab. 3:17–18). That way, our hope and joy are not based on how well things are going. They are based on Him.

I believe God is bringing His people into new a place of knowing Him. He is helping us discover what it really means to delight in Him, putting all other concerns aside and fixing our gaze on who He is. In that place, it doesn't really matter if you're in a barren wilderness or a season of fruitfulness. With all eyes on Him, everything else fades into the background. If we can get our hearts and minds into that place, we will discover the peace that passes understanding, the joy of His presence, His ever-present help in our times of need. This is really our greatest need, even more than what we accomplish for Him or the miracles we are able to experience. Joy in our circumstances is fleeting, but the joy of the Lord is our strength. Delighting in Him and experiencing the joy of His presence are primary. Everything else comes after.

Seeking and Finding Miracles

I'm not sure how many Christians have noticed the connection between walking in joy and experiencing God's wonders, but it's a powerful connection. Those who are able to delight in God above all else are finding Him immensely powerful and faithful in their circumstances. It's so good what He is doing these days. He sends His radiant ones out into the streets and sets them up for divine appointments with those who need a touch from Him. What He is doing is very exciting.

The Spirit is looking to awaken us to what He is doing in the kingdom. The whole earth is groaning for the manifestation of God's sons and daughters, and that means we must wake up to who we really are. We must know the inheritance we've been given. If we want to walk in wonders, we have to live in the joy of His presence.

How do we experience these things? Read what Jesus told His disciples about receiving the fullness of the Spirit:

> Keep on asking and it will be given you; keep on seeking and you will find; keep on knocking [reverently] and [the door] will be opened to you. For everyone who keeps on asking receives; and he who keeps on seeking finds; and to him who keeps on knocking, [the door] will be opened. Or what man is there of you, if his son asks him for a loaf of bread, will hand him a stone? Or if he asks for a fish, will hand him a serpent? If you then, evil as you are, know how to give good and advantageous gifts to your children, how much more will your Father Who is in heaven [perfect as He is] give good and advantageous things to those who keep on asking Him!
> —MATTHEW 7:7–11, AMP

God does not spoon-feed us. Spoon-feeding all the time is actually not very good parenting; when you give children everything they want all the time, you actually disempower them. They never develop a sense of responsibility or grow in their ability to solve problems. God is a much better father than any of us are as parents, and He doesn't want to treat us as infants who get their needs met without ever even asking or seeking the solutions. Instead, He awakens us to His invitations to get up and pursue what He is offering. He wants us to find joy in the things He has created us to do. He is calling us into a relationship of seeking and finding.

It would be impossible to list all the things God invites us to seek, but this lifestyle of miracles certainly qualifies.

He offers it to us freely if we will pursue it. But we have to remember to ask, seek, and knock, and many of us don't.

Think about some of the questions and attitudes we have that inhibit our seeking. Have you ever:

- Woken up in the morning emotionally tired and apathetic about the day

- Complained about what you're lacking or what's going wrong

- Been discouraged that breakthrough hasn't happened yet, at least not the way you expected

- Felt anxiety over how a situation is developing and how it might go wrong

- Constantly asked God questions such as "When?" "Why?" "How?"

- Waited for God to do something and wondered why He seemed to be completely silent or inactive

These are all symptoms of helplessness, even though God has already given help for these situations. In many cases we think the ball is in His court when really it's in ours. I think there is certainly a place for waiting on God—that's a huge part of faith, as exemplified by Abraham, Joseph, David, and many others—but sometimes God is waiting on us. And that is especially true in cases when He has already given a solution and we haven't accepted it yet.

For example, why wake up feeling helpless in the morning when God has already given everything pertaining to life and godliness, including His own divine nature (2 Pet. 1:3–4)? Why remain in sadness when He has already invited you into His presence, where there is fullness of joy (Ps. 16:11)? Why descend into a spiral of discouragement about your lack of breakthrough when God says that if you delight yourself in Him, He will give you the desires of your heart (Ps. 37:4)? Why struggle with anxiety about your circumstances when He has already said not to be anxious for anything because He will answer your prayers and give you peace (Phil. 4:6–7)?

In many cases we think the ball is in His court when really it's in ours.

In all of these things, we have a choice. We can get miserable and discouraged, or we can receive what He gives. We look to God and ask, "Why don't You do something?" And He looks to us with the very same question: "Why don't you do something? I've already offered you what you're looking for. Ask, seek, knock, and you will find. Enjoy in faith what I have promised before you even receive it, because I am faithful to do what I have promised and want you to live in joy of that reality now."

It seems that whenever God says something, the enemy chimes in with an alternative. When we're asking, seeking, and knocking, the devil's alternative is to sow seeds of hopelessness and invite us to a pity party. "Look what hasn't happened yet. Isn't that terrible? I know you must be so disappointed about that." But you have to refuse to go there. Follow David's example: "Bless the LORD, O my soul, and all that is within me, bless His holy name. Bless the LORD, O my soul, and forget not all His benefits" (Ps. 103:1–2, MEV). Tell your soul to delight in God no matter what is bothering you. Offer every care to Him with prayers of supplication and thanksgiving. Make your requests known and let His peace guard your heart and mind in Christ. These are not pious, theoretical possibilities. They are concrete realities to experience practically in real life. God has proven Himself in these things. We can receive them in confidence.

FINDING THE PLACE OF DELIGHT

At one point near the end of his exile, David and his men were hiding out among the Philistines. David had already passed up two opportunities to kill Saul and try to assume the throne on his own. He was faithfully waiting on God's timing. But one day during this wait in the wilderness, he and his men raided nearby enemy towns and came home to find their village of Ziklag burned and their wives and children kidnapped by Amalekites (1 Sam. 30). It was so devastating that David's own men—those who had been with him through years of distress and were ready for the ordeal to end—began talking about stoning him. It was a horrific moment of loss, as years of faithfulness to their leader seemed to have resulted in nothing but catastrophe. There seemed to be no victory in this wilderness. And they were holding responsible the leader who twice could have killed his enemy and didn't. In their grief, they wanted to kill David.

David inquired of God and received a promise that he could pursue the enemy and recover everything. But before he turned to God with a question, one brief statement tells us that David turned to God for something else: "David strengthened himself in the LORD his God" (1 Sam. 30:6, NKJV). It doesn't tell us how David strengthened himself, just that he did. In the middle of one of the worst crises of his life, when he could easily have lost heart and gotten stuck in depression, David turned his focus to God, entered His presence, and got strength. And from there, he got up and asked God for solutions and received them. Victory came, and joy was restored.

You will experience crises too, and there will be times in the wilderness when you get discouraged. But if you aren't coming quickly out of those places into absolute joy, you need to know that you can. You can strengthen yourself in God. You can draw aside from time to time and receive everything you need from the Father, just as Jesus did. God has already provided for your deepest needs, and He wants you to come and receive.

If you think that means, "I'll just go to worship and then hope something happens," God wants to rearrange your thinking. He wants you to come to worship because He is worthy, not to see something happen. He wants you to seek Him because He is worth seeking and deserves honor. He wants you to come with the attitude of David: "One thing I ask from the LORD, this only do I seek: that I may dwell in the house of the LORD all the days of my life, to gaze on the beauty of the LORD and to seek him in his temple" (Ps. 27:4). That is the place of absolute joy, no matter what else is going on.

> *You can be part of that army of people who say, "Yes, Lord, I'm choosing to follow You."*

There are times when I run out of words to describe how wonderful God is, and praises keep pouring out in my prayer language. They just don't stop. When you let go and decide you have no agenda other than to bless God and delight in Him, it doesn't get any better. What God begins to do is so extraordinary and glorious, it stirs up even more joy in you. He wants to take you on adventures and do beyond what you can ask or think, above even what your heart desires. You need supernatural joy to be able to handle what He wants to give. It's so, so good.

God wants us to experience sheer delight, but instead

of letting us simply wait until He brings it, He issues an invitation to seek His face. He has told us where this sheer delight can be found, but we have to get up and go after it. This delight is in His presence. And if you're not feeling it, then the answer isn't to sit back and wait. It's to keep asking, keep seeking, and keep knocking. Then it will be opened to you.

An army of people who decide in their hearts that they are going after God is now rising up. There is swift acceleration and promotion in the field in these days. You can be part of that army of people who say, as the disciples said centuries ago, "Yes, Lord, I'm choosing to follow You." That will require some discipline and diligence; I know that sounds like work, but it's what Paul told Titus about those who were preparing for ministry (Titus 3:8). God wants His army to set their faces like flint in His direction, refuse to be distracted, and lay hold of everything He has for them.

If you're feeling a bit under the foot of the enemy, that's not the truth. You have been created for fellowship with God. You are the head, not the tail. You're above, not beneath. Your circumstances don't dictate to you; you dictate to them. God wants you to lift up your head and step toward Him. Then He begins running toward you.

A Time of Refreshing

If you're in the middle of a transition right now—and many people are—you may be tired and longing for a rest. There are times when you've come too far to go back but don't know if you want to go forward. In those times, look to the Spirit who refreshes you. Let Him lift up your head. His yoke is easy and His burden light. He is with you, He is for you, and He has surrounded you with a great cloud of witnesses who are cheering you on. He is waking you up and reminding you of who you are.

God is looking for a mature bride, not an infant. It's time to rise up and say, "I'm going to bless You, honor You, worship You, and enter into Your joy. I'm going to receive what You have given me and celebrate it. When I'm concerned, I'm not going to whine and wonder when You'll come through. I'm going to ask for Your help and seek Your face." Mature faith doesn't lament and wallow in helplessness. It cries out, listens, hears, declares, and pursues.

Many people are sitting immobilized in sackcloth and ashes even though God has given beauty in place of ashes, joy in place of mourning, robes of righteousness and a garment of praise instead of filthy rags (Isa. 61:3). Your feelings may not match these gifts of beauty, joy, righteousness, and praise, but you have a choice. You can either be moved by what you feel or you can build your life on the truth. You can lament losses and be anxious for everything, or you can enter the joy of God's presence and be anxious for nothing. I've had the pity parties before, and they aren't fun. Even if people join you in the sackcloth and ashes, it's not a good experience. Getting up to bless God, honor Him, pray, receive, and declare is a much more fulfilling way to go.

The fun comes in God's presence—enjoying Him and experiencing His glory. When things aren't going well, we have the opportunity to bring Him an offering and delight His heart. The more difficult the circumstances are, the more joy you can have in delighting in Him. All heaven marvels when the church begins to rise out of pain and ashes, and the enemy gets very scared. You absolutely frustrate the plans of Satan when you refuse to sit in sackcloth and ashes. God comes in and lays a banqueting table before you in the presence of your enemy.

When Jesus heard the news about John the Baptist being beheaded, He went to withdraw, but because of compassion for others He instead ended up ministering to and initiating the feeding of five thousand men and their families (Matt. 14:13–21). The crowds had followed Him, and the disciples tried to send them home. But Jesus told His followers to feed them. Why? Because God lays a banqueting table before His people in the presence of their enemies. Jesus could have given up and talked about how awful and unfair John's death was. Instead, He reminded everyone of God's great love and kindness through a miraculous sign.

What would the enemy do with an entire army of people who couldn't be discouraged? What weapon would he have left if we believers chose not to let our circumstances dictate our sense of well-being? From his perspective, we would be untouchable.

> *Hold on tight to your Father, surrender your will to His, and follow His lead.*

The Word of God reminds us of who we are and what we have. So when circumstances confront us and try to convince us of how bad things are, we can look at the Word and say, "No, greater is He who is in me than he who is in the world" (see 1 John 4:4). We are reminded that we have been cleansed, sanctified, and made righteous before God. We are told that God is faithful, and He will accomplish what He called us to do (1 Thess. 5:24). We are called to wage war together with Him in the lion's den. And we are assured that if we believe Him, we will do the works He did and even greater ones. We have everything we need in God's Word and in the power of His Spirit not to fall prey to discouragement. We can freely delight in Him.

Nothing is impossible for God. He is faithful to answer

prayers, even while you are still praying them. He responds to those who delight in Him above all other desires. He lays before you a banqueting table in the presence of your enemies. He calls you out of the ashes and into the beauty of His presence, where there is absolute joy—and where wilderness ends and wonders begin.

HOLD TIGHT TO THE FATHER

Wilderness seasons don't have to be awful. In fact, these seasons are our greatest opportunity to grow and discover the joy and power of fellowship with God. It is actually the grace of God that allows us these times to prepare us for future promotion. During the times of wilderness and waiting, there is much we can do to gain the most out of the season. And there are valuable lessons that must be learned before we can move on. God knows how to tailor-make each wilderness we walk through to help us grow into the destiny He has for us.

My advice to you in the wilderness? Hold on tight to your Father, surrender your will to His, and follow His lead. His ways are better than yours, and He knows the areas of your life that need developing better than you do. Discover the truth that our call is to minister to God, and the opportunities to do that will continue to increase. Learn to be faithful with little and you will be empowered to be steward over much. The Father is even more interested in your future than you are. And your response in the wilderness will carry you into the fullness of everything He has prepared for you.

NOTES

CHAPTER 2
FINDING GOD IN THE PROCESS

1. Katherine Ruonala, "Faithful," *Faithful* (Brisbane, Australia: Katherine Ruonala, 2007), CD.
2. Katherine Ruonala, "Cover Me," *Faithful* (Brisbane, Australia: Katherine Ruonala, 2007), CD.

CHAPTER 3
THRIVING IN THE WILDERNESS

1. Katherine Ruonala, "Only You," *Faithful* (Brisbane, Australia: Katherine Ruonala, 2007), CD.
2. "What a Friend We Have in Jesus," by Joseph M. Scriven and Charles C. Converse, 1868. Public domain.
3. Katherine Ruonala, "Wandering," *Faithful* (Brisbane, Australia: Katherine Ruonala, 2007), CD.
4. Brother Yun, *The Heavenly Man* (Grand Rapids, MI: Kregel Publications, 2002).

CHAPTER 5
MAINTAINING INTEGRITY IN THE FACE OF INJUSTICE

1. Charles Spurgeon, *The Complete Works of Charles Spurgeon, volume 17*, Sermons 968–1027 (Harrington, DE: Delmarva Publications, 2013), viewed at Google Books.

CHAPTER 7
RECEIVING FROM THE GOD OF ALL COMFORT

1. Kathryn Kuhlman, "The Power of Love," CD.

CHAPTER 9
PRAISING IN THE STORM

1. "It Is Well With My Soul," by Horatio G. Spafford, 1873. Public domain.
2. The American Colony in Jerusalem, "Family Tragedy," Library of Congress, accessed May 19, 2015, http://www.loc.gov/exhibits/americancolony/amcolony-family.html.

3.   Spafford Children's Center, "History," accessed May 19, 2015, http://www.spaffordcenter.org/history.

CHAPTER 11
WAGING WAR WITH THE PROMISES

1.   Brainy Quote, "Albert Einstein Quotes," accessed May 19, 2015, http://www.brainyquote.com/quotes/quotes/a/alberteins 384440.html.

2.   Albert Einstein, *Cosmic Religion: With Other Opinions and Aphorisms* (New York: Covici-Friede Inc., 1931), 97.

ABOUT THE AUTHOR

KATHERINE RUONALA IS prophetic revivalist and conference speaker who brings a fresh word and impartation of God's Spirit. Katherine carries a strong prophetic and healing anointing and witnesses many signs, wonders, and miracles in her meetings. Her message reaches across denominational walls, and her ministry spreads the fires of revival in the hearts of all believers.

Katherine and Tom Ruonala are the founders and senior ministers of Glory City Church in Brisbane, Australia, and the international Glory City Church network (www .glorycitychurch.com.au). Katherine also hosts her own television program, *Glory City TV*, and has made appearances on *Sid Roth's, It's Supernatural!* and other programs. Katherine and Tom also serve as part of Harvest International Ministries apostolic team, and Katherine is the founder and coordinator of the Australian Prophetic Council (http:// australianpropheticcouncil.com.au). Katherine regularly travels and ministers in conferences around the world and hosts the annual Australian Prophetic Summit in her hometown of Brisbane, Australia. Katherine and Tom are happily married and have three beautiful children—Jessica, Emily, and Joseph.

To contact Katherine Ruonala Ministries, visit
www.katherineruonala.com
or e-mail info@katherineruonala.com

You may also like to write to
Katherine Ruonala Ministries
P.O. Box 1077
Springwood, Qld,
Australia, 4127

To invite Katherine Ruonala to speak at your ministry
please complete the form at
www.katherineruonala.com/invitations/

For information on Glory City Church
International Network or Glory City Church
visit www.glorycitychurch.com.au

To view live-streaming of our services and
archives of past services please see our YouTube
channel, www.youtube.com/glorygathering

To watch *Glory City TV*, visit www.glorycity.tv

To purchase additional Katherine Ruonala and Glory
City Church resources, visit www.glorycity.tv/product/

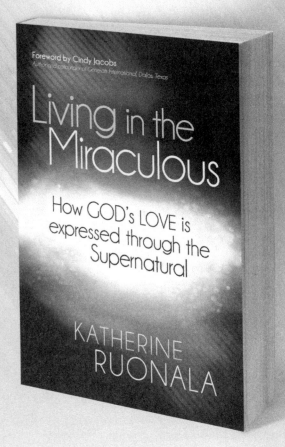